A HISTORY OF THE CANADA ASSISTANCE PLAN

1966 to 1996

by Kenneth Coward

ISBN 0-9698635-2-7
Printed by Skyway Printing
Hanover, Ontario
January 2000

Prime Ministers of Canada[1]
1966 to 1996

Rt. Hon.L.B.Pearson
April '63 to April '68
Photo by Ashley Cyippen Studio

Rt. Hon. P.E. Trudeau
April'68 to June '79
March "80 to June '84
Photo by Duncan Cameron

Rt. Hon. C.J. Clark
June '79 to March '80
Photo by Mia and Klaus

Rt. Hon. J.N. Turner
June '84 to September '84
Photo by Al Gilbert, C.M.

Rt. Hon Kim Campbell
June '93 to October '93
Photo by Denise Grant

Rt. Hon. M.R. Mulroney
September '84 to June '93
Photo by Ken Ginn

TOC

Rt. Hon. Jean Chrétian
October '93 to present
Photo by Phillipe Landreville

THE CANADA ASSISTANCE PLAN
1966 to 1996

CONTENTS

Pages

PREFACE

This study is mainly a history of the Canada Assistance Plan in federal, provincial and municipal Public Administrations. All quoted data information for fiscal years is verifiable from original sources, recorded by bibliographies footnoted. See the GLOSSARY of TERMS re "Fiscal years". Data detailed in the appendices indicate historical trends involving THE CANADA ASSISTANCE PLAN and other Social Security Programs; also, all sorts of budgetary expenditures are surveyed, selected from federal and provincial PUBLIC ACCOUNTS. Appendices VI & VII contain detailed records of expenditures and programs about Canada's significant historical contexts of social services and social security. And samplings of Metropolitan Toronto's municipal budgeting accounts selected from Metro's records are used in this study to analyze trends from 1966 through 1996. All data records in this study cover the years 1966 until termination of the Canada Assistance Plan in 1996. Some information about social services, and social security, in Canada since 1996, is also provided here. A HISTORY OF THE CANADA ASSISTANCE PLAN falls within many, many other histories, the dimensions of which can only be referred to here. But "INTERVENING VARIABLES", Chapter 2, extends into other histories.

The word "WELFARE" has historical roots in Canada. Records at the federal level still use the word "Welfare" to distinguish between Welfare Program Expenditures, Health Expenditures and Education Expenditures for Total Social Security Expenditures. And in Ontario, the General Welfare Assistance Act and Regulations is legislation governing "assistance" in the province. Ontario's history isn't about all provinces of Canada of course, but major programs, with which the Government of Canada became involved for cost sharing with Ontario, were also cost shared between the Government of Canada and the other provinces. Historically, the "Department of Public Welfare", created in Ontario in 1931, was Ontario's original department providing a variety of social services. Gross expenditure for the first year of the Department of Public Welfare in Ontario was $12,171,393. The net outlay was, $5,223,392., an amount lower than gross expenditures, because the department's programs were cost-shared between federal, provincial, and municipal levels; municipal contributions were made to Ontario for Mothers' Allowances; and the federal government subsidized Ontario's Old Age Pensions[2]. Footnote #2 refers to DECADES OF SERVICE, by Dr. Clifford Williams, "A History of the Ontario Ministry of Community and Social Services 1930-1980" which contains all sorts of informative history about social services' programs. (See review in APPENDIX XIII) My study here also includes historical notes from parts of my 1994 publicaton, THE WELFARE[3]. Whence many references here to WELFARE in this historical study of the Canada Assistance Plan. Agreements of the Canada Assistance Plan, in 1966, effectively coordinated arrangements between the federal and provincial governments. Legislation of the Government of Canada "assented to 15th July 1966" is titled as CHAPTER 45, "An Act to authorize the making of contributions by Canada towards the cost of programs for the provision of assistance and welfare services to and in respect of persons in need."[4]

To look back to the 1960s, the following speech provides a concise, yet comprehensive, history of the development of THE CANADA ASSISTANCE PLAN. I discovered the speech at Ontario's Archives which are located on Grenville Street in Toronto. I copied the words of the speech exactly as they were typed in the archival manuscript, but the format and the punctuation of the following edited copy is slightly different than the original. The speech by Norman F. Cragg, who was one of the original federal administrators of the Canada Assistance Plan, is reprinted here "As it was delivered at the Annual Meeting & Conference of the Ontario Welfare Council, May 17, 1966."

THE CANADA ASSISTANCE PLAN
by Norman F. Cragg

"It is customary for a speaker to express appreciation for the opportunity of speaking to a group as broadly representative, influential and well informed as this one. I am able to express that appreciation very sincerely, for the Ontario Welfare Council has long since established an enviable reputation, not only for the functions it performs, but more particularly for the quality of its Annual Meetings, and for the thoughtful and challenging way in which it uses these occasions as a forum for considering current social issues and setting goals for the future. I am honoured to have been asked to give the opening address, and I appreciate the opportunity to present the Canada Assistance Plan to you and to put forward some of its implications as I see them.

It is typical of the forward planning that goes into Ontario Welfare Council projects that the request for this address should have been made on November 9th, 1965, a good six months before the Conference. It seemed reasonable to assume, at that time, that the Canada Assistance Plan would, by now, have been enacted by Parliament particularly since April 1st, 1966 had been set as the date upon which the plan would become effective.

For a variety of reasons, the Plan has not yet come before the House, other than in the form of a resolution although we are hopeful that it will be enacted very soon.

You will appreciate, therefore, the dilemma that I face. As a public servant, I am limited in what I can say to the aspects of the Plan referred to in public statements made by the Prime Minister and the Minister of National Health and Welfare. While a number of statements have been made, they deal in broad terms with the proposal and do not go into the details of its actual operation in which many of you are interested. Under these circumstances, perhaps the most useful approach for me is to put the development of the Canada Assistance Plan into context, and consider the potential impact of its provisions on welfare programs.

- -

To appreciate the Plan fully, one should look at it from two points of view. The first sees it as a milestone in the sequence of public assistance measures, while the second recognizes it as one of a number of social and economic measures designed to improve employment opportunities, to deal with the causes and effects of poverty and, through increased opportunities, to reduce dependence on public assistance.

It can be said, with some measure of truth, that the Canada Assistance Plan represents a return to an earlier tradition of general assistance. For the past half century, we have been in the era of categorical assistance which began with the development of mothers allowances programs during and subsequent to the first World War when legislative action was taken to recognize the special requirements of a particular, and obviously needy group in the population. The introduction of Old Age Pensions in 1927, blindness allowances in 1937 and old age assistance in 1952, extended this concern to other readily identifiable groups of persons. Action followed for the disabled in 1954 and with the enactment of the federal Unemployment Assistance Act in 1956 recognition was given to the need for more adequate assistance to persons whose need arises because of unemployment. By this time the elements of adequate public assistance legislation existed, but we suffered from the fact that need was not met through a variety of uncoordinated measures, most of which tended to identify the cause rather than the fact of need.

Along with the growth of public assistance there have also developed a series of social insurance measures such as workmen's compensation, unemployment insurance, and, most recently, the Canada Pension Plan. Taken with the universal programs of old age security pensions, and family and youth allowances, it can be said that Canada possesses the essential elements of a broad and soundly based approach to social security.

The developments to which I have referred came about because of a number of influences and events, not least of which were the representations made by interested groups of citizens and voluntary organizations. With the development of local, provincial and national welfare councils, orderly, systematic and informed planning and coordination has become possible. Thus the Canada Welfare Council, in 1957, was able to draw upon the resources of many councils across Canada and other voluntary groups as well as public bodies in preparing its well-known and influential policy statement on

- -

"Social Security for Canada". In his statement on the Canada Assistance Plan made in the House on April 6th, 1965, the Prime Minister referred particularly to the wide support for a comprehensive program of public assistance that had been expressed by welfare organizations and authorities including the Canada Welfare Council.

There were a number of cogent reasons for the various expressions of concern and demands for improvement. Among the limitations in existing programs across Canada that have been identified are the following:

1. Discrepancies exist between various programs which often result in

discriminatory and differential treatment being accorded to persons depending on the category into which they fall. The result is not only inconsistencies in the treatment of persons in need, but also complicated administration and duplication of effort. Having said this, however, I must immediately qualify by recognizing that there may be varying conditions or sets of circumstances in which applicants for assistance find themselves, which may justify differential approaches to the test of need. A case for differences in treatment could thus be made, for example, for persons experiencing short-term unemployment, the aged, or those who are sick or disabled.

2. The variety of programs, each directed to specific categories of individuals, has tended to militate against the development of a consistent and integrated approach towards meeting the needs of the family as a unit.

3. There has been insufficient recognition of the need for such essential elements of a public assistance program as health care and welfare services.

4. And, finally, the number and qualifications of staff has been substantially less than that needed to properly administer the various programs, and to introduce the qualitative aspects necessary if preventive and rehabilitative measures are to be taken.

- -

I have made these background comments to emphasize a number of points relevant to the development of the Canada Assistance Plan.

1. That while the essentials of a sound public assistance program had been reasonably well established by 1957, it was clear that some gaps in terms of coverage remained to be filled, that integration of the separate programs was essential, and that the concept of public assistance needed to be broadened to include a concern for prevention and rehabilitation as well as amelioration.

2. That planning councils and other organizations saw the need for change, extension and improvement and, through the national planning body, presented a carefully prepared brief that represented a consensus of their thinking and that of business, professional and labour leaders in the country.

3. That this thoughtful, well presented and authoritative document is

acknowledged as an influence in the creation of the Canada Assistance Plan.

4. And, finally, that this series of events illustrates the influence that responsible social planning bodies can have, and underlines the importance of insuring that organizations, such as the Ontario Welfare Council, are able and willing to interpret and document the need for change.

I suggested a moment ago that the Plan should also be seen in the context of a whole range of social and economic measures designed to deal with problems of poverty. You will recall that in 1965, the Prime Minister announced that the government was "developing a program for full utilization of our human resources, and the elimination of poverty among our people." He indicated that the program would include improved measures for regional development, the re-employment and training of workers, the re-development of rural areas, the provision of assistance to needy people, the renewal of areas now blighted and congested in our cities, and the establishment of new opportunities for young Canadians. Besides strengthening and broadening measures within the federal sphere, the program would be designed to co-ordinate them more effectively with provincial programs. A number of specific measures were identified, most of which now are or soon will be in effect.

- -

We in the field of social welfare have long since recognized that the provision of assistance does not, by itself, have the positive effect required if the recipient is to be helped to overcome the problems he faces. At the same time it has been recognized that positive action must be taken in a variety of forms and through a number of different but related measures. In this context, the role assigned to the Canada Assistance Plan is evident in its emphasis on the provision of health care and welfare services, to the end that persons in need can be constructively helped to become as self-supporting as possible.

Thus far I have attempted to set the stage for a better understanding of the Canada Assistance Plan. Now I want to deal with the questions - what is the Plan, and how will it operate?

The Plan is a joint federal-provincial measure, and it has been the subject of intensive federal-provincial discussions extending over the past two years. Assuming that all provinces sign agreements, the Plan will take effect to the extent that provincial legislation makes this possible. It is proposed that it become retroactively effective to April 1st of this year.

As you know, responsibility for the administration of public assistance programs rests with the provinces. It is up to them to design programs to meet their particular circumstances, to set their own conditions of eligibility and rates of assistance, and to determine the form and extent of the welfare services they provide. The Canada

Assistance Plan will provide financial support to them in improving and extending their programs of assistance and welfare services.

The impact of the Plan will not be immediately apparent because it breaks new ground in a number of ways and must take into account other federal legislation. More-over, the text of the Bill even when carefully read by the well-informed will not provide a very descriptive indication of the measure. It may be helpful, therefore, for me to comment on major elements or aspects of the Plan, nine of which are identified:

- -

1. The Plan provides, first, for the development by the provinces of comprehensive, integrated public assistance programs. There are, at present, four pieces of federal-provincial public assistance legislation, - the Unemployment Assistance Act, the Old Age Assistance Act, the Blind Persons Act, and the Disabled Persons Act. The Unemployment Assistance Act will remain in force for a relatively short time, but we expect a rapid transfer to the Plan of the groups now covered under it. The provinces may, at their option, either continue to provide benefits under the three other acts, or discontinue acceptance of applications under these programs and provide assistance for persons otherwise eligible for benefits under them through the Plan. In instances where recipients are transferred, however, it is the intention that benefits provided to them shall be at least comparable to those presently enjoyed, and when one adds other benefits such as health care made possible through the Plan, it is likely that recipients will be in a significantly more favourable position than if they had remained under the old program.

2. While the Plan provides that the provinces can move at their own pace in integrating the existing federal-provincial programs to which I have just referred, it also makes it possible for them to integrate other programs which in some provinces have been set up to assist particular groups of people. In this connection, the Plan will, for the first time, extend federal sharing to costs of mothers allowances which have been excluded under the existing unemployment assistance program. In making some $27 million of additional funds available to the provinces in this way, the federal government is hopeful that they will be able to make improvements in their existing and developing programs.

3. A third important element in the Plan has to do with health care. In accordance with the principle that assistance should be adapted to the needs of the individual, the Plan will provide that the federal government will pay half of the cost of health care services for persons in need. Most provinces have developed various measures through which public

assistance recipients now receive health services, but I think it would be correct to say that in no province have these been fully comprehensive and in some they have been quite limited.

- -

The scope of the Canada Assistance Plan respecting health services for the needy is very broad. For example, it may include medical and surgical services, nursing, dental and optical care, including dentures and eyeglasses and prosthetic appliances. Federal sharing will continue in these areas until such time as there is a federal-provincial program available covering the general population. The sum estimated at $20 million that the federal government will make available to the provinces for health care services to persons in need will help them to extend such services beyond the present level and thereby eliminate some of the exclusions which are now characteristic of the programs in many provinces, exclusions which have often caused hardships to many individuals.

It will however, be up to the provinces to decide the extent to which they will take advantage of the health care provisions proposed under the Plan and it may take some time before any given province can make the financial, administrative and service provisions necessary to provide additional health care services along the lines and to the extent that will be possible within the scope of the Plan.

4. A fourth element, and one which is generally considered to be among the most important and constructive aspects of the Plan, is the support it will provide for strengthening public assistance administration and for improving and extending welfare services. This is in recognition of the fact that if public assistance programs are to have a positive effect they must have incorporated into their administration provisions for services which are designed to assist individuals and families in avoiding the need for assistance and in regainding their maximum potential for self-support. In the absence of these services public assistance programs are concerned with financial need, but do not deal effectively with the problems that cause the need.

- -

For the purposes of the Plan, welfare services are intended to include services that have as their object the lessening, removal or prevention of the causes and effects of poverty, child neglect or dependency on public assistance. They include such things as counselling, assessment and referral services, homemaker and day care services, community development, staff training and development, and program research and evaluation. Contributions will be made for these services where they are provided by provincial and municipal welfare departments and, under certain circumstances by voluntary agencies. The method of reimbursement, and consequently the approach to be taken in providing for voluntary agency participation, will be set out precisely in the Act, and you will no doubt wish to carefully examine those sections that deal with this matter when the Bill is made public. The important point, however, is that under the Canada Assistance Plan, the federal government will support the provinces in the development of a social rehabilitation approach which, through a variety of services, will seek to assess the needs of the individual, and through counselling, the provision of welfare services, and carefully worked out referrals to training, employment and related community services, undertake to help him to achieve independence wherever this is possible.

As most of you know, the Canada Assistance Program is not the first venture of the federal government into the provision of assistance with the costs of enlarging and improving welfare services. Since 1962 the Welfare Grants Program has provided, partly through the provinces, partly through direct grants, assistance with the costs of training welfare personnel, expanding welfare services and of research pointed toward the improvement of such services. However, this assistance has been available only on a project basis under an annually renewable Order-in-Council authorizing the expenditure of limited funds. The Canada Assistance Plan will enable federal assistance to the services it involves on a continuing statutory basis without financial limits.

- -

5. The Plan will also break new ground in sharing in the costs of assistance and services provided to children in the care of child welfare agencies. Children under the age of 18 have been excluded under the blind and disabled persons programs, and only a few so-called "assistance type children" were covered under the unemployment assistance program. The coverage of children is consistent with the aim of the Plan to reverse the years of segregation and categorization - a trend already apparent in many provinces. The fact that welfare services and child welfare services are provided by the same field staff in many provinces makes the inclusion of children highly desirable, their exclusion illogical and administratively complex.

6. A sixth element of the Plan is the basis upon which eligibility for assistance will be determined. The Plan will call for a needs test, which

takes into account budgetary requirements as well as resources, rather than a means test as the method of determining eligibility and the amount of assistance payable. This approach has been criticized on the ground that the needs test involves unnecessarily complicated and cumbersone procedures. In my view there are ways of avoiding this kind of problem. In any event, we know of no other method by which the particular circumstances of an individual in need can be more appropriately assessed and met.

There will be no ceiling on the amount of federal sharing in assistance and no exclusions in respect of the persons for whom assistance may be required.

7. A seventh element in the Plan is the provision it makes for sharing in work activity projects for persons who have unusual difficulty in obtaining or keeping employment because of environmental, personal or family problems and who are not able or prepared to utilize the various training and rehabilitation services available to the general population. Support will also be provided for work activity projects used to provide employment in sheltered surroundings for persons who, because of physical or mental handicaps, have little potential for gainful employment in the ordinary labour market. Where work activity projects are set up there will be close liaison with the federal department responsible for the vocational training and vocational rehabilitation programs to ensure no duplication. The projects will serve to meet the needs of individuals who have been unable to take advantage of existing programs. As such they will provide an element of flexibility hitherto lacking.

- -

8. The eighth feature of the Plan is the provision it makes for federal contributions towards the cost of assistance and welfare services for Indians on reserves. This support will be provided under the terms of a special federal-provincial agreement and services are to be extended only with the consent of the Indian bands. The purpose of this provision is to enable the progressive extension of assistance and welfare services to Indians on the same basis as to the general population and to secure access to such services without reference to place of residence. I should point out that provinces will not be asked to enter into these special agreements as a condition of signing an agreement under the Canada Assistance Plan. We hope, however, that where they are not able to do so immediately they will be able to indicate the point at which they can undertake such an extension.

9. A ninth feature concerns the relationship of the Plan to other income maintenance programs, in particular the Canada Pension Plan. While the latter will eventually go far towards meeting income requirements for contributors and their families who find themselves without their normal means of support because of retirement, disability or widowhood, it is recognized that for some time to come, until benefits build up under the pension plan, the pensions for which persons will be eligible may be insufficient to meet the needs of those who lack other resources. Further, it is recognized that, for some, supplementation will always be needed. A third need for assistance will arise for those persons who have not been covered by the pension plan. Thus, the intention is that social insurance and social assistance measures will be co-ordinated to insure that no person will lack the necessities of life.

- -

10. The last point I wish to make has to do with the role of the federal government in relation to the Plan. It is clear that the implementation and administration of assistance programs is the responsibility of the provinces. The major role of the federal government will be to channel federal funds to enable provinces to more adequately discharge their responsibilities in this area.

The department of National Health and Welfare, however, recognizes its responsibilities for assisting provinces in other ways. It will, therefore, be prepared to provide consultive services in such fields as public assistance standards, accounting and audit, welfare institutions, family and child welfare, services for the aged, community development, research and staff training. In this way we hope to be able to provide advice and assistance designed to help ensure that the extent and quality of welfare services is reasonably consistent across Canada.

I understand that following my remarks a panel will comment on the Canada Assistance Plan and will consider some of its implications. This procedure frees me from the obligation of attempting to point out all the implications as I see them, and makes it possible to give special attention to three or four of the the issues that I think will be of special interest to you.

The Canada Assistance Plan is a program that extends beyond the federal and provincial governments to the local community - to its municipal welfare department, its child welfare agencies, its welfare institutions, and to its voluntary health and welfare agencies that provide services to persons in need. It is, in part, because of its relevance to community welfare agencies that the enactment of the Plan is being awaited with more than usual interest by such agencies, as well as by provincial welfare departments.

- -

The emphasis given by the Plan to prevention and rehabilitation implies that all available community resources should be brought to bear in dealing with problems of poverty and dependency. Just how these resources will be utilized will, of course, be for the provinces to determine.

This approach has two important implications:

1. It could prove to be a significant extension of previous coverage of public assistance programs and provide an important preventive element in such programs, and

2. It creates a means whereby voluntary agencies can be appropriately reimbursed for services provided to persons in need or likely to be in need.

You will recall that the definition of welfare services is very comprehensive, in that it extends not only to preventative and rehabilitative services for individuals, but also to community development services. The possibilities, therefore, for involvement of voluntary agencies are quite extensive, and it remains for means to be worked out which will enable them to play their most effective and appropriate roles.

It is not possible to make a clear-cut distinction between the responsibilities of government and the responsibilities of voluntary agencies in the welfare field. Even if this were practicable and desirable at a given time, conditions and requirements change too quickly for such a distinction to have any long-term validity. We can agree, I think, that the responsibility of government is to establish the broad general principles of social programs and to underwrite a large share of their cost. Community agencies can operate within these broad outlines, providing complementary, ancillary and new services, and generally supplying the personal element that reflects individual and community concern in the field.

- -

While I have indicated that the Canada Assistance Plan is designed to provide for voluntary agency participation under conditions to be determined by the provinces, I am sure you will realize that such participation is not without its hazards. Greater opportunities for services, yes. But the acceptance of public funds must, if the public authority is to discharge its functions responsibly, entail some measure of supervision and control and perhaps some loss of flexibility. Beyond what point does such supervision go before the agency ceases to be voluntary, in the sense that it is directed by citizens acting in a voluntary capacity?

A related problem may arise. With the increasing demands on voluntary funds, the temptation will exist for community chest budget committees to reduce allocations for agencies financed in part by public funds. Yet the objective of the Canada Assistance Plan is to channel new funds into programs to help extend, develop and improve them. Will it be possible to consider such funds as extra money to be added to existing budgets?

A second important implication has to do with the needs test, one of the underlying principles of the Plan. The needs test approach will help to ensure that an individual's actual needs are identified, and assistance tailored to those needs. For example, the test may disclose that a family head has sufficient resources to meet his current requirements, but that he is unable to provide for an emergency that calls, let us say, for homemaker services. The needs test approach can be used to meet such special and particular circumstances, and hence is more realistic, more generous and more helpful way of meeting need.

This approach can be especially beneficial to the aged, whose requirements usually extend well beyond the need for a given amount of money. Homemaker services, day care services, meals on wheels, counselling, health care services, comforts allowances, - the need for such services can be identified through the intake process, and funds made available to support them.

- -

However, a certain stigma has come to be attached to the idea of the needs test. Consequently, many proud and independent people resist the idea of applying for assistance. I hope that these negative ideas can be largely overcome. This call for positive interpretation, and, just as important, positive administration that convinces recipients that assistance and services are given, not grudgingly, but as a right. The applicant should fully expect to be treated in a manner that respects his dignity, his integrity and his sense of worth.

A third implication, which I mention but leave to others to deal with, has to do with the number and quality of staff needed to fully and effectively implement the programs envisaged by the Canada Assistance Plan. This calls for accelerated programs of recruitment, training and deployment that go far beyond present efforts. I may add that the Department of National Health and Welfare is examining how it may contribute more effectively to this process, particularly through improvements in the Welfare Grants Program.

My final point concerns public assistance within the total framework of social security. As the Canada Pension Plan matures, as comprehensive measures are developed in the field of health, and as the various manpower programs begin to more adequately achieve their objectives, we hope that the need for public assistance programs will decline. This decline would no doubt be further hastened if Canada were to adopt an income maintenance program involving the guaranteed annual income, an approach now receiving a good deal of public attention. But as far ahead as anyone can now see, we will require a strong, flexible public assistance program with emphasis on welfare services. The Canada Assistance Plan will help to ensure that it is an effective program, and that in its rehabilitative approach to people, and its preventative approach to poverty and dependency, it can be a significant element in the total complex of measures designed to help people realize their full potential as participating citizens of Canada.

- -

You will appreciate that I have not been able, in the time available to me, and because the Plan is not yet enacted, to provide full details of its various provisions. I have, however, attempted to set out the major outlines, and to emphasize its most important points. To set the stage for the discussions to follow, it may be helpful to summarize its essential features.

1. The Plan provides for the development of a single comprehensive integrated program of public assistance, based on a test of needs.

2. It helps to eliminate present gaps by providing federal funds for mothers allowances, health care, child welfare, and welfare services.

3. It recognizes the need for adequate numbers of appropriately qualified staff, by providing federal funds for staff training and development.

4. It recognizes the need for program research and evaluation, and so helps to ensure that public assistance programs can be continuously assessed and appropriately modified.

5. It emphasizes, for purposes of federal sharing, the concepts of prevention and rehabilitation. It thus helps to move public assistance programs beyond the relief of need, to the position of being able to deal constuctively with causes and effects of poverty."

ADDENDUM regarding subsequent history since 15 August 1991:

The Supreme Court of Canada ruled that the federal government acted within its powers by enacting Bill 69 of the Financial Administration Act. In effect, the Court ruled that the federal government can restrain its share of funding of the expenditures under the Agreements of the Canada Assistance Plan, as specified in Bill 69, for British Columbia, Alberta and Ontario.

FOOTNOTES RE THE BACK OF FRONT PAGE AND THE PREFACE

1. THE PRIME MINISTERS OF CANADA, Presented by the HOUSE of COMMONS and the NATIONAL ARCHIVES of CANADA. © Minister of Supply and Services Canada 1994 Cat.No.:SA2-247/1994, ISBN 0-662-60272-2

2. DECADES OF SERVICE, A history of the Ontario Ministry of Community and Social Services, 1930-1980, by Clifford J. Williams, Copyright 1984, The Ministry of Community and Social Services, 134 pages, ISBN 0-7743-9004-2.

3. THE WELFARE: A Concise Archival History of Social Services, by Kenneth Coward, printed and bound in Owen Sound, Ontario, Canada, Stan Brown Printers, 1994, 90 pages. ISBN 0-9698635-0-0

4. CHAPTER 45, Canada Assistance Plan, 14-15Elizabeth II. Roger Durhamel, F.R.S.C., Ottawa 1966.

INTRODUCTION

We're involved here with available historical information about Canada's Public Administration of government, mainly for the years 1966 to 1996, including the Canada Assistance Plan from 1966 to 1996. But record keeping with government information involves no end of problems. (see the GLOSSARY, regarding "Record keeping"). Canada's central government, whether by records keeping resources, or by advanced public services know-how, attends to more information about people than do other Canadian governments. Minute by minute, in Canada, the central government co-ordinates all sorts of data, from all parts of the nation, about the people of Canada; whereas other governments of Canada rarely co-ordinate among each other about the peoples of the different provinces and territories. And within each province and territory, data information maintained by each government, about peoples within the provinces, isn't comparable to the data information maintained by the central government about all people in Canada. (See APPENDIX VIII about FINANCIAL INFORMATION, PUBLIC ACCOUNTS OF CANADA. Also see Appendices IX and X, regarding availability of provincial and municipal historical records from Ontario and from Metro Toronto, sampled for data information.

What should be a dominant rationale for writing a history of social services? Should the endeavour be self seeking? Should it be educational? Should motives for writing history intend to affect social changes? All such questions are beyond the historical concentration of this book which is mainly informative about publically funded social services of the Canada Assistance Plan; in CHAPTER 3, co-production issues and programs of social services are also referenced. Co-production Services, provided by voluntary or private agencies, are usually beyond government administration, but many co-production programs are publically funded and accountable to legislated regulations. Many agencies were providing social service programs before the programs became funded or subsidized by governments. In other words, such agencies and their programs, weren't created as privatization of government programs. And some social services, now under government jurisdiction, such as Children's Aid Societies, were originally controlled by private agencies. Histories of many co-production agencies, and the social services programs they provide, are usually very different than histories of government departments and the programs provided by the departments. For detailed histories of social services, and for outlines about how some private programs evolved into services provided by the Government of Ontario, see DECADES OF SERVICE, A history of the Ontario Ministry of Community and Social Services[1].

The present historical study of THE CANADA ASSISTANCE PLAN, inspired in many ways, so to speak, doesn't attempt to resolve all sorts of concepts. My research and writings of the text simply carried on in the midst of all varieties of intervening concepts. Which isn't an unusual condition of work. For examples, most research and writings carry on in the midst of unsettled, background concepts which are often buttressed by contradictory sayings such as "followers of good words" vs "followers of good deeds", or "game play in the name of the game" vs "game play for the sake of the team". Nor did I realize a need for history about social services by the fact that significant history about the Constitution of Canada is needed. I'm not qualified to attempt any approach to Constitutional issues, and neither are most other people not qualified. Whom among students, politicians and the public at large can explain the Charter of the Constitution of Canada? Whom can explain the absence of the Province of Quebec as a signatory of the Charter of Rights? Whom can explain that Codified Law in Quebec is different than Common Law in the rest of Canada, and that legislative enactments in the Province of Quebec are primarily written en francaise. All such explanations can only be made by Constitutional experts and by lawyers. Only experts can determine how Canada can exist as a nation. Yet all sorts of passionate opinions about Canada persist among students, politicians and the public at large. Many of the opinions fret that Canada may fall apart, that our basic networks may be torn asunder, although Quebec has always been separate from the rest of Canada. What's the context of the Constitution of Canada? Will the Constitution and Charter likely be in status quo for the foreseeable future?

In 1995 a "REVIEW ARTICLE, by Keith G. Banting about the social policy review" of SOCIAL SECURITY IN CANADA, noted significance in studies of social policy. According to Banting, "the study (of SOCIAL SECURITY IN CANADA) reveals much about the contradictory pressures shaping contemporary public policy in Canada."..."From the outset, the social security review was caught in the tensions existing among three separate agendas: the reform of social policy, the reduction of the federal deficit, and the accomodation of Quebec within Canada[2]." (NOTE: SOCIAL SECURITY STATISTICS' catalogues, extensively referenced in APPENDIX VII, are separate publications, different than the SOCIAL SECURITY IN CANADA publication which Keith G. Banting reviewed.)

And quoting from THE WELFARE, my earlier study mainly about the 1970s and 1980s in "A Concise Archival History of Social Services" from Chapter 1, "Idealists, of Ontario's history, although they represent links to our past, are not significant to the understanding of modern, government operations. But linkages from the past do affect our present[3]." "What will happen?" and "What should happen?" I've been asked, by persons who know I've been researching the history of the Canada Assistance Plan. The questions are about the termination of the Canada Assistance Plan, and it seems to me answers to "What will happen?" are covered by daily news. Answers to the question, "What should happen?" are more difficult to determine. To effectively attend the present and future of public administration, I've briefly reviewed selections from bibliographies of research.

When I became involved with the notes and readings for this study about social services, I became preoccupied with some usages of ill defined words in other studies, words such as "understandings", "theories", "consultations" "concerns"; it seems to me, my study of The Canada Assistance Plan can only randomly comment concretely, as I do, about such word usages, especially regarding "concerns". And the question of concern, "What should happen?", it seems to me, can also be randomly commented upon. Each individual reader here who researches among other studies I've briefly reviewed, will find meanings and significance pertinent to themselves. But a GLOSSARY OF TERMS is offered in this study to amplify meanings of words used; though it doesn't answer concerns of the question, "What should happen?" To critically examine that question would require a far more extensive study than the present work, and ultimately also reflect upon mankind's attrocities committed in response to such questions as, "What should happen?".

FOOTNOTES TO THE INTRODUCTION

1. DECADES OF SERVICE, A History of the Ontario Ministry of Community and Social Services, by Clifford Williams. Copyright, 1984 the Ministry of Community and Social Services, ISBN 0-7743-9004-2

2. CANADIAN PUBLIC ADMINISTRATION, The Journal of the Institute of Public Administration of Canada, Summer 1995, #2, p. 283 a "REVIEW ARTICLE by Keith G. Banting, of The Social Policy Review: Policy Making in a Semi-Sovereign Society," pp. 283-290

3. THE WELFARE, A Concise Archival History of Social Services, by Kenneth Coward; printed by Stan Brown Printers, Owen Sound, 1994, ISBN 0-9698635-0-0

CHAPTER 1:
THEORIES OF PUBLIC ADMINISTRATION

Can a rationale of history understand short term conditions and circumstances? For example, assuming that stabilization in the market for goods and services is the fairest and most equally distributed condition among a population, can stabilization be known? Can inflation be known? According to Statistics Canada, inflation can be known, although its conditions need to be vigilantly reviewed. Nevertheless, destabilized inflationary conditions can't always be anticipated. Approximate stabilization in all day market places is desireable for most people who manage their personal affairs on budgets. But as supplies, merchants and buyers shop for the best price, they define each other, exchanging goods and services, where conditions develop which aren't actually games but are dance like make-believe, coached and or choreographed amidst some wit and cunning. Poor people and unemployed people aren't involved in this sort of make-believe. Neither are wealthy, wealthy people involved.

Accumulations of data information, pertaining to Public Administration, Economics and History, are expected to be accurate, of course, in the midst of infinite directions whence cometh and goeth information. Economists handle market activities in concepts of supply and demand, under microeconomic and macroeconomic, economic theories, including attentions to government policies about involvements in market activities. News media rarely report extensive details about everyday markets and market places of the majority of people; and notwithstanding meager sorts of stability of the poor and unemployed, news about food banks is rarely reported. Economic conditions can take hold whereby inflation enters the market and the marketplace. This personification of inflation suggests many metaphors which can also be imagined. And if you've known inflation, your imagination is much more vivid than are the imaginations of persons who haven't known inflation. Economics as a discipline would likely define comments about imaginations as undisciplined and irrelevant, written as though economists and policy makers have nothing else to do than attend to imaginations of the public. While effects of depressions and inflations, and other upheavals, brought devastations and sad memories to Canadians through the depression of the 1930s and inflations of the 1970s & 1980s. See the study of the C.D. Howe Institute by D. Laidler and W. Robson 1993, THE GREAT CANADIAN DISINFLATION[1].

Inflation destabilizes conditions of persons in need, hence social services, attempting to serve persons in need, increase allowances of assistance, and supports of welfare services, to provide some stability in the midst of increased and increasing costs. All sorts of inferences might be concluded from rising expenditures on social services, or rising expenditures for any other budgetary accounts, of for examples, in the Public Accounts of Ontario or in Public Accounts of Canada. Persons who lived through inflations of the 1970s and 1980s won't be surprised to see jumps in the records of 1970s expenditures by multiples of 3, tripling 1980s expenditures; and then, multiples of 2 in the expenditures of 1980s, doubling expenditures' records of the 1990s.

Such increasing expenditures aren't all attributable to inflation though. Other sorts of tragedies, too many to outline by a word for every sort of tragedy, affected Canadians through every span of time of the 20th century, including devastations, sometimes outlined by a single word, "war". And another word associated with tragedies in communities is "rancor". The conditions and circumstances, briefly outlined here, are approached in many different ways in studies of Public Administration, Economics and History. The elements are usually handled as social facts, although each study approaches the social facts differently. Some studies are reckless, and some outrageous. Some mild, some moderate and some radical. A country like Canada has been able to allow all sorts of political expressions on all sorts of varieties of informed and uninformed opinions. Politicians sometimes allow their pollsters, and other opinion advisors, to be identified, although most political opinions aren't required to be acknowledged, as to sources of the opinions.

In APPENDIX I, my review/report of PUBLIC ADMINISTRATION IN CANADA, SELECTED READINGS, edited by W.D.K.Kernaghan and A.M.Willms, 1971, found Dwight Waldo involved with problems of "understanding" about public administration. He offered definitions, but qualified them, stating, "There is nothing wrong with such definitions - except that in themselves they do not help much in advancing understanding[2]." Dwight Waldo originally wrote the article for his book, THE STUDY OF PUBLIC ADMINISTRATION, in 1955. So in this sense we can   at least establish time frames about his problems of definition and "understanding." Also, we can elaborate his definitions by saying, the Canada Assistance Plan of Public Administration didn't exist in 1955. But of course other Public Administration programs were studied by Dwight Waldo in the mid 1950s, whence his problems of definition.

To be more completely informed about earlier decades and the theories of years before 1970, readers can look back at a recommended book for public administration courses of the 1970s containing studies from earlier decades, PUBLIC ADMINISTRATION IN CANADA: SELECTED READINGS[3], Several critical theoretical studies are included in the text, Chapter One, "Public Administration and Organization Theory". It's a good start for information about theories in organizations, although most administrators might be indifferent as discovered in a study of theory among public administrators. (see a brief review in my Chapter 4 here of James Iain Gow's study, "Members'survey on theory, practice and innovation in public administration," 1987-88,)[4]. Nevertheless, theories continue to be part of social sciences, and in a history of social services it's pertinent to refer to theoretical studies.

Compelling issues about theories of management and organizations also draw us to more current studies presented in PUBLIC ADMINISTRATION IN CANADA, A TEXT, by Kenneth Kernaghan and David Siegel, 1987, Second Edition,[5] - reviewed here in APPENDIX II; the 1995 Third Edition under the same title is also reviewed here in APPENDIX II[6], Students studying public administration courses, while attending to public administration as an occupation, incline to anticipate advances in theories; impressed by history, from theories about scientific management to theories about organizational humanism, or from theories about closed systems compared to theories about open systems. Additions and amendments in the history of theories of organization might be considered as advances. Theories presented in the 1971 text are almost the same as theories presented in the 1987 text with additions and omissions in the 1987 text. And, theories presented in the 1987 text are almost the same as theories presented in the 1995 text but with additions and omissions in the 1995 text. For example, of an addition, in the 1995 text, a section about "TQM" "Total Quality Management", refers to a management style which involves employees of manufacturing enterprises in shared management concerns about the qualities of their products[7].

For students who want to follow issues of personnel management, see Kernaghan and Siegel's Second Edition in the 1987 text, Chapter 22, especially their bibliography on "COLLECTIVE BARGAINING."[8] Most of this Chapter 1, "THEORIES OF PUBLIC ADMINISTRATION", reviews writings about Public Administration; more such reviews are in "APPENDIX I" and "APPENDIX II". Also, comments about theories extend from here into Chapter 4, "METAPHORS OF PUBLIC ADMINISTRATION ".

FOOTNOTES TO CHAPTER 1. THEORIES OF PUBLIC ADMINISTRATION

1. THE GREAT CANADIAN DISINFLATION, by David E.W. Laidler and William B.P. Robson, C.D. Howe Institute, Toronto,

2. PUBLIC ADMINISTRATION IN CANADA: SELECTED READINGS; by W.D.K. KERNAGHAN and A.M. WILLMS, second edition, METHUEN PUBLICATIONS, Toronto, 1971. 481 pages.

3. Ibid

4. CANADIAN PUBLIC ADMINISTRATION, The Journal of the Institute of Public Administration of Canada, Fall 1989, Volume 32, Number 3. pp. 382-406. "Member's Survey on theory, practice and innovation in public administration" by James Iain Gow.

5. PUBLIC ADMINISTRATION IN CANADA, A TEXT, Second Edition, by Kenneth Kernaghan and David Siegel, published by Methuen Publications, Toronto 1987, 642 pages, 1987 ISBN 0-458-80650-1

6. PUBLIC ADMINISTRATION IN CANADA, A TEXT, Third Edition by Kenneth Kernaghan and David Siegel, published by Nelson Canada, Toronto, 1995, ISBN 0-17-604187-7

7. Ibid

8. PUBLIC ADMINISTRATION IN CANADA, A TEXT, Second Edition, by Kenneth Kernaghan and David Siegel, published by Methuen Publications, Toronto 1987, 642 pages, 1987 ISBN 0-458-80650-1

CHAPTER 2
INTERVENING VARIABLES

Readers want to know from whence writers or concepts are from, so aside, I've included commentaries which seem to me to be significant in a study of THE CANADA ASSISTANCE PLAN, including information concerning social services of governments and of agencies outside governments. Also, historical data and some explanations about all social security statistics are included here. However, we're involved mainly with A History of the Canada Assistance Plan from a different slant, approaching many sorts of data information after data has been reported in other sources. Not original source records from services' offices which aren't available for this sort of study, although pertinent sorts of data information reports are presented here from reported government expenditures about The Canada Assistance Plan. Comparisons and questions about government expenditure' data are infinite though, and massive presentations of data information are more descriptive and comparative than analytical. Examples of the variety of data information with which CAP was involved can be reviewed in Appendices VII, VIII, IX & X. From municipal committees and councils, and provincial committees and legislatures, and in federal committees and the Parliament of Canada, the Canada Assistance Plan was among all governmental concerns and issues, of which this history attempts a significant survey.

Before the Government of Canada became experienced with billion dollar expenditures, Gross National Expenditures for selected years 1939 to 1958, were (in millions of dollars) as follows, (add 000 to each following expenditure)[1]

1939	1946	1950	1955	1956	1957	1958
$5,636	$11,850	$18,006	$27,132	$30,585	$31,773	$32,509

By the time 1966 arrived, Net Federal Expenditures were beyond $7 billion. In the interval, of course, many Social Security Programs had been established. See APPENDIX VII, SOCIAL SECURITY STATISTICS for outlines about social security programs including the CANADA ASSISTANCE PLAN. So in effect, history of expenditures was altogether different earlier, although there had been programs for pensioners, and the unemployed, and other social services in the years preceding the 1960s. When net federal expenditures extended to billions of dollars, each federal department was establishing exceptional history as yearly spending, in each department, exceeded earlier, total all Canada yearly expenditures.

The following data information was obtained from Statistics Canada. The same information is also recorded in Population information of APPENDIX IV. This column presents population data from Censuses of Canada. In-between years, between each Census, census estimates were used, but details about those estimates aren't noted. Population data here isn't intended to imply nor to infer correlations between growth of population statistics with growth of expenditures. However the population of Canada does affect Canada's expenditure budgets. More detailed information is provided in APPENDIX IV, involved with data about employment/ unemployment and other labour force statistics.

Actual and estimates of data information by Statistics Canada are usually reported by calendar years.

POPULATION STATS CANADA
(APPENDIX IV) Ages 15 yrs and over

1966	13,083,000
1967	13,444,000
1968	13,806,000
1969	14,162,000
1970	14,528,000
1971	14,872,000
1972	15,186,000
1973	15,526,000
1974	15,924,000
1975	16,323,000
1976	17,124,000
1977	17,493,000
1978	17,839,000
1979	18,183,000
1980	18,550,000
1981	18,883,000
1982	19,177,000
1983	19,433,000
1984	19,681,000
1985	19,929,000
1986	20,182,000
1987	20,422,000
1988	20,690,000
1989	20,968,000
1990	21,277,000
1991	21,613,000
1992	21,986,000
1993	22,371,000
1994	22,717,000
1995	23,027,000
1996	23,352,000
1997	23,687,000

See pp. 87 & 92 population data - all ages.

Here follows a history of data information about Federal Net Expenditures for the years, 1966 to 1997. The column on the left records expenditures' totals for years 1966 to 1997 for all federal spending. The right column, "PUBLIC ACCOUNTS", indicates the last year records of federal expenditures were updated.

	NET FEDERAL EXPENDITURE	PUBLIC ACCOUNTS EXPENDITURES' RECORDS AS OF
1966	$7,659,000,000	1969-70
1967	8,718,000,000	"
1968	9,798,000,000	1970-71
1969	$10,738,000,000	1972-73
1970	11,931,000,000	1973-74
1971	13,182,000,000	1974-75
1972	14,841,000,000	1975-76
1973	18,340,000,000	1976-77
1974	22,551,000,000	1977-78
1975	29,213,000,000	1978-79
1976	33,978,000,000	"
1977	39,011,000,000	1980-81
1978	42,902,000,000	1981-82
1979	46,923,000,000	1982-83
1980	53,422,000,000	1988-89
1981	62,297,000,000	"
1982	74,873,000,000	"
1983	88,521,000,000	"
1984	97,120,000,000	1992-93
1985	$109,628,000,000	"
1986	111,528,000,000	1994-95
1987	116,673,000,000	"
1988	125,406,000,000	"
1989	132,840,000,000	"
1990	142,637,000,000	1996-97
1991	151,353,000,000	"
1992	156,389,000,000	"
1993	161,401,000,000	"
1994	157,996,000,000	"
1995	160,785,000,000	"
1996	158,918,000,000	1996-97
1997	149,793,000,000	" 2

The above is the sort of data with which the Minister of Finance was involved as federal debt overwhelmed expenditure budgets of the Government of Canada. According to the Minister of Finance, the Hon. Paul Martin, the "debt to GDP ratio" was rising relentlessly over two decades. (see Chapter 4)

The following pertinent, data information is presented here to emphasize historical concentrations about the CANADA ASSISTANCE PLAN. The following amounts were total federal transfers by Canada to the provinces and territories.

CANADA ASSISTANCE PLAN
TOTAL FEDERAL PAYMENTS[3]

1969	$355,930,000.
1970	458,529,000.
1971	599,082,000.
1972	727,288,000.
1973	768,211,000.
1974	824,276,000.
1975	$1,068,569,000.
1976	1,396,432,000.
1977	1,617,948,000.
1978	1,558,546,000.
1979	1,702,545,000.
1980	1,911,412,000.
1981	2,285,849,000.
1982	2,656,771,000.
1983	3,219,642,000.
1984	3,657,328,000.
1985	4,020,447,000.
1986	4,284,506,000.
1987	4,440,312,000.
1988	4,729,586,000.
1989	5,108,392,000.
1990	5,502,554,000.
1991	6,602,136,000.
1992	6,801,792,000.
1993	7,382,653,000.
1994	7,880,571,000.
1995	7,947,480.000.
1996	7,885,351.000.
1997	152,493.

SOCIAL SECURITY STATISTICS catalogue FOOTNOTES, NOTES: #3 of TABLE 434, notes, "Payments under the Young Offenders Agreement have been included for 1980-81 to 1987-88".

	NET FEDERAL EXPENDITURE[4]	C.A.P. FEDERAL PAYMENTS Footnote[5]	POPULATION STATS CANADA (APPENDIX IV)
1966	$7,659,000,000		13,083,000
1967	8,718,000,000		13,444,000
1968	9,798,000,000		13,806,000
1969	$10,738,000,000	$355,930,000.	14,162,000
1970	11,931,000,000	458,529,000.	14,528,000
1971	13,182,000,000	599,082,000.	14,872,000
1972	14,841,000,000	727,288,000.	15,186,000
1973	18,340,000,000	768,211,000.	15,526,000
1974	22,551,000,000	824,276,000.	15,924,000
1975	29,213,000,000	$1,068,569,000.	16,323,000
1976	33,978,000,000	1,396,432,000.	17,124,000
1977	39,011,000,000	1,617,948,000.	17,493,000
1978	42,902,000,000	1,558,546,000.	17,839,000
1979	46,923,000,000	1,702,545,000.	18,183,000
1980	53,422,000,000	1,911,412,000.	18,550,000
1981	62,297,000,000	2,285,849,000.	18,883,000
1982	74,873,000,000	2,656,771,000.	19,177,000
1983	88,521,000,000	3,219,642,000.	19,433,000
1984	97,120,000,000	3,657,328,000.	19,681,000
1985	$109,628,000,000	4,020,447,000.	19,929,000
1986	111,528,000,000	4,284,506,000.	20,182,000
1987	116,673,000,000	4,440,312,000.	20,422,000
1988	125,406,000,000	4,729,586,000.	20,690,000
1989	132,840,000,000	5,108,392,000.	20,968,000
1990	142,637,000,000	5,502,554,000.	21,277,000
1991	151,353,000,000	6,602,136,000.	21,613,000
1992	156,389,000,000	6,801,792,000.	21,986,000
1993	161,401,000,000	7,382,653,000.	22,371,000
1994	157,996,000,000	7,880,571,000.	22,717,000
1995	160,785,000,000	7,947,480,000.	23,027,000
1996	158,918,000,000	7,885,351,000.	23,352,000
1997	149,793,000,000	152,493.	23,687,000

The above columnar histories of data information joins the three above separate sets of historical data, namely, Expenditures data from the PUBLIC ACCOUNTS OF CANADA, and C.A.P. data from SOCIAL SECURITY STATISTICS, and Census data from STATISTICS CANADA. Of course, C.A.P. data is included within the data of the NET FEDERAL EXPENDITURES' column.

Comparisons within each set of the above data, and between each set of data, prompt all sorts of questions. Many of the begged questions can't be answered here. Statistical data information about the CANADA ASSISTANCE PLAN is published in SOCIAL SECURITY STATISTICS catalogues - see APPENDIX VII. And see Table 360 in the catalogues for "Total Federal-Provincial Cost-Shared Program Expenditures".

Comparative historical data from the Province of Ontario, showing net provincial expenditures, compared with data about Ontario expenditures, for programs shareable under the Canada Assistance Plan, is presented in APPENDIX IX. And, Metro Toronto expenditures records compares the municipality budgets with shareable social services data in APPENDIX X. Data information from the Province of Ontario, and from Metropolitan Toronto, are used as examples of provincial and municipal expenditures in this study. The Canada Assistance Plan had similar, cost-sharing agreements, as with the Agreement with Ontario, with all provinces across Canada.

Governed times, of course, involve more than measured times as political organizations affect affairs of government, and as politicians affect political organizations. The following politicians were leaders in government before, during and after data accumulated which I've quoted from Canada's Total Yearly Budgetary Expenditures, including expenditures of the Canada Assistance Plan of the Government of Canada.

BEFORE -
    P.M. Louis Ste. Laurent
    Finance Minister Walter Harris
    P.M. John Diefenbaker
    Finance Minister Donald M. Fleming

DURING -
    P.M.s   Lester Peason, Pierre Trudeau, Joseph Clarke, John Turner, Brian Mulroney, Kim Cambell, Jean Chretien.
    Finance Ministers Walter Gordon, Mitchell Sharp, Edgar Benson, John Turner, Donald MacDonald, Jean Chretien, John Crosbie, Alan MacEachen, Marc Lalonde, Michael Wilson, Gilles Loiselle, Donald Mazankowski, Paul Martin.

AFTER -
    P.M. Jean Chretien
    Finance Minister Paul Martin

Before closing this chapter about "Intervening Variables", I must insert the following quotations from an economics text,

" 'GNP is measured in market prices'. A doubling of all outputs with price held constant has the same effect on measured GNP as a doubling of all prices with outputs held constant. Yet these two changes will have very different effects on human well-being."

" 'ADJUSTING NATIONAL INCOME MEASURES': Misinterpretations of any single measure of aggegate economic activity are inevitable if that measure is used to serve all purposes. Different measures are needed for different purposes: to measure the demand for labor, an atomic missile is as important as a commercial jetliner and go-go dancing as important as school teaching; if concern is with human well-being, a different view may be appropriate. To estimate government tax revenues money incomes are needed, not real purchasing power. However...etc'" (the authors continue with regard to variables of aggregate economic activity.)

The authors of the above quotes also go on to 'Adjusting for price changes: "Constant Dollars" ', and 'Adjusting for population changes: Per Capita'. Economists in general have all sorts of variables in mind in almost anything they say or write. I'm not attempting to be an economist by quoting them; but by using the above quotes, I've brought economics into this chapter about "Intervening Variables" from an ECONOMICS text, "Chapter 27, Key Variables of Macroeconomics: Employment, Prices, and National Income"[6]. To carry the digressions somewhat further, for purposes of anyone following economic history, "GNP" isn't popularly referred to nowadays, except historically about Gross National Product. For examples of Gross Domestic Product, "GDP", see catalogues of SOCIAL SECURITY STATISTICS' where Table 1 utilizes socio economic data, described in detail, regarding Total Social Security Expenditures, Gross Domestic Product, and Total Government Expenditures. (Also see Appendices in the catalogues for detailed comments about the SOCIAL SECURITY STATISTICS)[7]

Logic, mixed with whatever logic needs, to bear upon public affairs, isn't likely to be more effective in the 21st century than logic has been in the 20th century. Unless, of course, technology brings logic into wider application to public affairs. No pretence of knowing hidden possibilities about logic here intended. But interpretations thereof, about histories, written before computer technology was widely available, would have been very different had historians used word processors and other technological aids for their writings. It seems then, historically, conditions of intervening variables and significance were earlier affected differently than are modern intervening variables and significance. Of course, generally speaking, historical writings are also judged according to times and places and to agreeability or disagreeability. But to wander into all such phenomena would be to wander into a bunch of questions which only philosophy could ultimately handle. Philosophers would probably perceive attitudes of agreeability and disagreeability among all sorts of other attitudes. I proceed with an attitude of creative criticism, and I try to be logical and to avoid attitudes of grumpy criticism.

FOOTNOTES TO CHAPTER 2. INTERVENING VARIABLES

1. CANADA 1959, Prepared in the Canada Year Book Section, Information Services Division, Dominion Bureau of Statistics, Ottawa, the Queen's Printer, Ottawa 1959, Catalogue Number CS 11-203/1959.

2. PUBLIC ACCOUNTS OF CANADA (see APPENDIX VIII)

3. SOCIAL SECURITY STATISTICS CANADA AND PROVINCES, 1968-69 to 1992-93, 1970-71 to 1994-95, 1995-96 to 1996-97 (3 recordings of Table 434), published by authority of Minister of Human Resources Development Canada, and .. available from (C) Minister of Supply and Services Canada. Cat. No. MT90-2/17-1993, & MT90-2/17-1995, ISBN 0-662-62742-3; but 1996 & 1997 data of Table 434 is from the internet address: link from the National Site, Home Page at http://www.hrdc-drhc.gc.ca/cgi-bin/AT-Nationalsearch.cgi

4. PUBLIC ACCOUNTS OF CANADA (see APPENDIX VIII)

5. SOCIAL SECURITY STATISTICS CANADA AND PROVINCES, 1968-69 to 1992-93, 1970-71 to 1994-95 and 1995-96 to 1996-97

6. ECONOMICS by Richard G. Lipsey, Gordon R. Sparks, Peter O. Steiner,"Chapter 27, Key Variables of Macroeconomics: Employment, Prices, and National Income" pp. 459-460, Harper and Row Publishers, New York, Evanston, San Fransisco, London; 1973
    ISBN 0-06-044014-7

7. SOCIAL SECURITY STATISTICS, CANADA AND PROVINCES, 1970-71 to 1994-95 published by authority of the Minister of Human Resources Development Canada, and is available from the Minister of Supply and Services Canada 1994. Cat. No. Cat. No. MT90-2/17- 1995, ISBN 0-662-62742-3

CHAPTER 3
CO-PRODUCTION

My writings aim for attentions of common sense rather than philosophy, although this present historical study of the Canada Assistance Plan indicates philosphical perimeters in studies of social services where most modern philosophers would say, "Experience determines understanding". Similarly this study isn't particularly involved with "understanding" as enduring and underlying conditions of knowledge.

All organizations co-produce among other organizations. In modern, urban civilizations, co-production is everywhere, including enterprises of all sorts co-producing with each other, and with governments; and governments of all sorts co-produce with each other and with enterprises. Everyone in many ways depends on others. Communications by way of Post Offices, FAX, couriers, and computer E-MAIL; transportation networks, manufacturers, farmers, educators, medical professions and workers; all these and many, many other networks are inter-dependent on each other in co-production. Yet, not everyone who's able to be employed is employed. Many commentaries about unemployment ridicule, or infer blame on governments, or departments and agencies of governments, for high rates of unemployment. Ridicule of government is perhaps widely used in the USA, and so advocates in Canada, acting on behalf of the unemployed, might reason that if ridicule works in the USA, where rates of unemployment are much lower than rates of unemployment in Canada, ridicule should also work in Canada. Whereas, in Canada in the heat of ridicule, among opposing sides, all sorts of antagonisms are likely to be turned on. Turning instead to Northrop Frye, his many references to Biblical imagery include, "On the demonic side of animal imagery are, as a rule, beasts of prey, like the wolf, the enemy of the sheepfold."[1] Governments of course aren't always innocent shepherds of sheepfolds in the midst of ridiculing conflicts. (see "Ridicule" in the GLOSSARY OF TERMS). A published multi-faceted article suggests that Canada has been under a great change, and jobs won't be like jobs of the past. Very few people will have one job for many years. Most people will have many jobs through their lifetimes. So, the multi-faceted manifesto proceeds to recommend how people should prepare themselves for many jobs through their lifetimes. The advice to job seekers is similar to historic manifestos, such as the Communist Manifesto of Karl Marx. But Marx at least offered an explanation about forces of history which were shaping conditions of working people, whereas the modern manifesto offers no explanation as to what is determining the changing lives of working people, except that everything is going to change often. That explanation existed long before now, in the saying, "Nothing's more certain than change itself." For readers wanting to know more about Marx, I defer to Northrop Frye. The INDEX of THE GREAT CODE indexes 8 pages referring to "Marxism" and 4 indexed to "Marx".

No doubt about it, unemployment won't go away by not talking and writing about, and doing something about, unemployment.And no doubt, news columnists and writers know something about the arts of communication in bringing issues into public consciousness. I'm not an artist of communications, but a book such as, <u>A</u>

HISTORY OF THE CANADA ASSISTANCE PLAN, is concerned about unemployment, and most of the information in the book is from government sources. Most organized efforts on behalf of unemployed persons, historically, have been carried out by government programs as governments became more and more involved mainly with day to day urban affairs. Rationalized government programs intend to be accountable, but innuendos, inferences, suggestions of causal connections, and all sorts of other random commentaries put more hurdles in the ways of concerted efforts of government programs. All this isn't to suggest that commentaries of columnists back off, but rather to suggest to artists of communications, regarding commentaries about unemployment, why not focus on agencies which are most likely able to be pertinent to unemployed persons, as well as focusing on inappropriate spending of government funding to get the unemployed employed. (See inappropriate spending of government funding in APPENDIX XVII). A pertinent job finding agency, advertising locally in Grey County, used an ad in a local newspaper, THE FLESHERTON ADVANCE.

JOB FINDING CLUB

Working together to find employment
Available for unemployed individuals who are job ready
and need assistance in finding employmment opportunities.
PRIORITY WILL BE GIVEN TO THOSE PARTICIPANTS WHO ARE
CURRENTLY RECEIVING EMPLOYMENT INSURANCE BENEFITS OR HAVE
RECEIVED BENEFITS IN THE PAST THREE YEARS, OR RECEIVED
MATERNITY OR PARENTAL BENEFITS IN THE PAST FIVE YEARS.

Learn new job search techniques that work, and discover how to tap the hidden job market.
Learn to prepare informative and impressive resumes, covering letters and calling cards that get results.
Expand your network of contacts for employment.
Obtain access to the Internet, Computers, Faxing,
Telephones, and more...
Up to date resources are available for interviews resumes, job searching ideas and employer research.
Between 75 and 80% of the participants will be employed within 3-6 weeks.

THE JOB FINDING CLUB
Annesley United Church, 82 Toronto Street South
(Hwy #10), Markdale
Starts September 16 and runs until Oct. 4, 1996
For further information or to register, please call
JBJ EMPLOYMENT SERVICES INC.
(519) 923-3437
Sponsored by Human Resources Development Canada[3]

A pamphlet in 1997/98 as follows was distributed by the "Y"

NEED A JOB?

We'll Help You Get One

THE FAMILY "Y"
CAREER AND EMPLOYMENT
PREPARATION PROGRAM

"Employment Counsellors are available by appointment to assist you:" (services of the counsellors are not quoted here but are outlined in the pamphlet)

"For those of you who meet eligibility criteria, a training incentive could help you get your foot in the door with an employer. If you have little or no work experience, or if you need to develop job skills relevant to your career goals, on the job training is a good way to learn those skills. In the past participants have found jobs"... (jobs are listed in the pamphlet but aren't quoted here)

"Our resource centres have books, publications and software available for you to use to conduct your research, form your plan and begin your job search." (resources are listed, and addresses of resource centres are listed in the pamphlet)

"Workshops are offered regularly on the following topics:
* Job Search Techniques
* Resume Writing

Workshops or other topics may be scheduled based on interest and need. All workshops are offered free of charge."[4]

"Serving Grey and Bruce Counties
Office Locations In:

Owen Sound   Hanover
648 2nd Ave. East   299 10th St.
(519) 371-9222 or   (519) 364-3163
1-800-265-3711

Unemployment rates sharply declined after such ads.

FOOTNOTES TO CHAPTER 3: CO-PRODUCTION

1. THE GREAT CODE THE BIBLE AND LITERATURE, by Northrop Frye, published by the Penguin Group, Penguin Books of Canada Limited, 10 Alcorn Avenue, Toronto, Ontario, Canada, M4V 3B2 ISBN 0-14-012928-6 260 pages, p.150

2. Ibid

3. THE FLESHERTON ADVANCE, Box 280, Dundalk, Ontario, Canada N0C 1B0

4. Owen Sound Y.M.C.A., 648 2nd Ave. East, (519) 371-9222

CHAPTER 4
METAPHORS OF PUBLIC ADMINISTRATION

References to metaphors here neither intend to conform to, nor to parody, Northrop Frye's scholarly writings about literature's metaphors. In this chapter, we reference modern organizations such as the Y.M.C.A. (i.e. the "Y") where "Purpose" has been its dominant preoccupation throughout Y.M.C.A. history in Canada since the 1850s. But through the years, experience became emphasized moreso than did belief systems. Whereas, early in the history of stated purposes of the "Y", adherence to literal biblical attitudes and beliefs was required. Since early beginnings in Canada, laymen and personel of the organization, were mainly male. As programs developed, Y.M.C.A. branches, with lay Presidents and Boards of Directors, were served and advised by "General Secretaries". "Y" Board Committees for Physical Education, Boys Work and Youth Work were served and advised by "Program Secretaries". In the 1950s, the Y.M.C.A. was concerned about its history of work among conditions known to Social Workers as "individual needs", "group needs", and "community needs"[1]. Through the 1970s and 1980s, the "Y" became more business-like, while becoming involved in co-production with Public Administration; "Y" personnel became CEOs, Presidents and Managers of Y.M.C.A. branches; and laymen became Chairmen of Boards and Chairmen of Committees. And girls and women became more extensively involved in programs and administration of the Y.M.C.A.

Not to assign possession of the word "will" in the name "George Williams", the originator of the Y.M.C.A., but his efforts in London, England, in the 19th century, became recognized, as did the efforts of other persons of "will". Such as Saint Marie among the Hurons, in early explorations among aboriginal peoples of Ontario, and Norman Bethune, practicing medicine in China in the 1930s, and it's certain they'd no longer hold the respect given them today if their work wasn't adaptible to change, allowing the Y.M.C.A., Canadian aboriginal peoples, and the practice of medicine in China to adjust as needed. Of course, many other agencies such as the Salvation Army and St. Vincent de Paul could also be acknowledged historically. More should be said here on the subject of "will". My above comments about the Y.M.C.A. and other agencies perhaps lead into my attempt to approach the subject, although Northrop Frye, a writer far more qualified, whose writings I've quoted extensively from his book THE GREAT CODE, doesn't overtly mention the subject of "will" in his study of the Bible and Literature. Most people leave the subject to philosophers. Some staff persons of the Y.M.C.A., whom had studied philosophy, could refer to sources which attend to the subject of "will" extensively, but at any sort of "Y" seminar or staff retreat of the "Y" in the decade of mid-twentieth century the subject of "will" wasn't approached in agendas. However, discussions among groups could include comments about Protestants who were inter-confessional unlike Catholics who attended confessions before a priest. According to Northrop Frye's comments, about Augustine's writings of CONFESSIONS, Augustine's "systematic presentations of doctrine are balanced against the emphasis on experience in the *Confessions*."[2] So the roots of the subject aren't too different, whether by Protestants or by Catholics. But that's about as near to consensus as the subject becomes, as Protestants split on any such subject between denominations, and Catholics split on any such subject between orders of the Catholic Church.

Like waves on stormy shorelines, phenomena break upon social services and upon services co-productive with social services, contrary to public administration and public will, sometimes inexplicably, which may be understood some day. Much of what we now know about social phenomena was beyond our understanding not many years ago, so we're led to anticipate greater understandings hence. But none of us will be "Phantoms of the Opera". Different disciplines of knowledge, such as economics, sociology, philosophy and public administration, will continue to view social phenomena most times separately, sometimes interactively, but never omnisciently.

Public consultation has become more established in some organizations since earlier public administration studies as outlined in Chapter 1. Usages of the word "consultation" however are similar to usages of the words, "understanding", "theory", and "unemployment" none of which are very clear usages. For example, Clifford Williams' study about <u>DECADES OF SERVICE</u> refers to changes in public thinking which occurred in the 1960s. "The participation of each interested person became an ideal of social action, consultation with the local community a rule, decentralization a goal, dispersion a virtue." p. 88.[3]

Much of the data and other research information used in this study was found in resources of the Robarts Library at the University of Toronto. Most of UofT's vast resources wouldn't be referenced for this history study of course. For example, fictional experiences on the campus with spirits and ghosts, as in writings from Robertson Davies at Massey College, and about myths he constructed at UofT; <u>MAN OF MYTH</u> is the title of his biography. My research experiences should be more actual than mythical to study <u>THE CANADA ASSISTANCE PLAN</u>. But occasional digressions are in my actual notes, for examples in APPENDIX XVIII and CHAPTER 5, about "MEDIA", from my research at the UofT library. And comments about Northrop Frye's studies, included in my writings, sometimes use poetic liberty, admittedly, when quoting Frye.

The overwhelming data in financial information at the end of the millenium and the beginning of the 21st century is the data of public debts in Canada. (see the "GLOSSARY OF TERMS" here, about Debts and Deficits etc; and see APPENDIX VIII for data about deficits and public debt). Coincidental with the growth of public debt in Canada has been tremendous growth in the expenditure side of government. Coincidental with tremendous expenditures growth of Canada's federal government has been expenditures growth among all levels of government, including provincial and municipal. Some persons, as passengers in motor vehicles, are oblivious of what's going on outside of the inside space of the vehicle.

I assume that those persons also travel through a history oblivious about what's going on outside the history. Overwhelmed by public debt, it seems that politicians and bureaucrats created finance-centric history as a screen from the workings of apocalyptic government. Borrowing the following portentious quotes from Northrop Frye, but not to draw non-pertinent commentary into the present study, "Man creates what he calls history as a screen to conceal the workings of the apocalypse from himself."[4] Northrop Frye, himself, wouldn't likely approve of using his writing in the context where I quoted him. As a matter of fact, he provided a sort of damage control in the introduction to THE GREAT CODE, in writing, "The theory of language has revolutionized so many approaches in psychology, anthropology, and political theory, to say nothing of literary criticism itself, that no one can any longer regard the humanistic concern with language as separable, or even distinguishable from other concerns. In many respects this simply opens up a new field of ignorance for me, and in any case many seminal questions in contemporary criticism would overcomplicate this introduction (i.e. Frye's "introduction" to his book) and must be left for later discussion[5]. In many places in his book, he refers to usages of "royal metaphors", for example, ' "to boost the prestige of dictators, "Hitler is building roads across Germany".'[6] The usages of "royal metaphors" thus were to Frye's youthful annoyance, and I'd expect he'd be annoyed if he were identified with a "royal metaphor" as an Auditor General of expenditures and the ways of government. And, although he referenced "royal metaphors" in many other ways, analytically, throughout his study of the Bible, he wouldn't likely have appreciated a metaphorical identity as Auditor General of the Bible. Nevertheless, conditions of "this is that", of interest in an auditor's review of financial records, aren't all that far fetched from "this is that" conditions of interest in Northrop Frye's review of Biblical records.

Northrop Frye quotes William Blake who said, "The Old and New Testaments are the Great Code of Art." So from Frye's book title and sub-title, THE GREAT CODE, "THE BIBLE & LITERATURE", and by reading the book, it can be realized he analyzed the Bible, and he often explained biblical contents and meanings by using other sources as required. For examples, Frye used the biblical story of Jonah's problems in the Whale to explain Job's problems with the Leviathan. And he used another source of literature about a heroine, Andromeda "who is already inside her leviathan". "Here we have the structural pattern behind any number of displaced versions in romance, in which a hero has to make a perilous journey into a place of great danger where the heroine is held."[7] For persons wanting more information about the Leviathan, Frye's book indexed the monster 7 times.[8]

Northrop Frye approached his writings analytically, working among and upon language, types, myths and metaphorical thinking and usages. He didn't personally view these conditions as literal prescriptions for living, but he did view them as arising from life on earth, as in the Bible's "uniting of the poetic and the concerned".[9] Especially metaphorically. Of course, metaphors of hell refer to an afterlife. Metaphors are thought to be not real, but according to Frye, old and new metaphors arise again and again as life becomes confused. Impressed by Frye's writings and his analysis of all sorts of historical information, my writings of history about the Canada Assistance Plan is inclined to look at historical contents analytically, including my reviews of THE PUBLIC ACCOUNTS OF CANADA. Frye observed, "Social sciences are based entirely on the sense of the need to observe the community of observers."[10] Observers of THE PUBLIC ACCOUNTS OF CANADA and growing government debts through the 1980s, are concerned that expenditure budgets in Canada could someday be dominated by deficits as debts extended into the 1990s. While the debt remains and was growing, people realize debt problems won't be solved until after deficits have been reduced to zero. (see my "GLOSSARY OF TERMS", regarding Debts and Deficits etc). My Glossary of Terms put here for definitions aren't as encompassing though as Northrop Frye's definitions; about language, for example, distinguishing "verbal magic" and "energy common to words and things, though embodied and controlled in words."[11] However, Frye was cautious, as I am, in reflections upon man's illusions, such as those of early astrology, "Even astrologers now could hardly accept astrology on the old causal basis of "influence", assuming that some physical substance emanates from constellations billions of miles away. The assumption is that the world is set up in such a way that there is a pattern of coincidence between configurations of stars and human lives that can be systematically studied". To carry the digression further, he acknowledged, "I didn't find any consistent astrological symbolism in the Bible, but there are many allusions to divination in it...emphasis on sevens and twelves in the Book of Revelations", (re seven planets and twelve signs of the Zodiac, "perhaps"). "Hence these numbers would suggest, more than others, a world where time and space have become the same thing. But correspondence does not seem to be the central thing that the Bible is saying about the relation between man and nature."[12]

Metaphors of classical organization theories cite Herbert Simon's study of specialization, unity of command, span of control, and organizational efficiency according to process, purpose, clientele and place. The theories don't work; all these mentioned terms aren't static while their meanings are constantly changing. And in the midst of discontinuities and weak theories, values of efficiency and effectiveness of management carried on, allowing for changing conditions and terms of reference, because acknowledged, organizational values were efficiency and effectiveness; notwithstanding later studies which refer to new values in public service. (see Kenneth Kernaghan's article in the IPAC Journal, CANADIAN PUBLIC ADMINISTRATION, Winter 1994, "The emerging public service culture: values, ethics and reforms")[13].

It's a good thing we have enduring Acts, Regulations and Policies as functioning organizations terminate. Musings about organizations and management may seem to be fascetious nonsense, sometimes even mischief, but observe carefully the history of classical organization theory and its aftermath.

"Pre-Christian writings about management subjects may be found, such as Kautila's ARTHASASTRA, translated by T.N. Ramaswamy in ESSENTIALS OF INDIAN STATECRAFT....; Plato's REPUBLIC.....; THE OLD TESTAMENT; more recently, Gibbon's DECLINE AND FALL OF THE ROMAN EMPIRE.......; and Machiavelli's THE PRINCE..... all treat with familiar management topics such as the chain of command, the span of control, and the specialization of labor."[14].

More up-to-date writings concerning theory are contained in articles of CANADIAN PUBLIC ADMINISTRATION, A Journal of The Institute of Public Administration of

Canada. An article by James Iain Gow, surveyed opinions of Senior Public Servants in Canada, whose "replies appear to support the impression that Canadian senior executives place higher value on their role as policy adviser than on that of manager"..."Deputy Ministers who replied to the questionaire of the Lambert Commission said that administrative management was important, but that policy competency was more important than managerial competency in the appointment process." Further, according to James Gow, the common point of view of the public service, "Is indifferent if not hostile to theory and does not rely much on reading for its inspiration .....There may be thousands of occupations in the public service, but the profession is government. This fact is seen in the references to politics as one reason why adaptations take place more often than rational planning, why reforms undertaken only partly succeed and why theories are not applicable in practice".[15]

See more about metaphors and theories in the following;

a. PUBLIC ADMINISTRATION IN CANADA: SELECTED READINGS, 1970 includes many theoretical analytically, critical studies about organization and management[16].

b. PUBLIC ADMINISTRATION IN CANADA: A TEXT 1987 handles all theories similarly to the above, with some varying usages; (eg. "person-centredness" became "humanism"). Very few differences, compared with the 1970 analysis of theories, were added to the 1987 text. (see APPENDICES I & II) The 1987 text reveals that Ontario's Government in the 1960s and 1970s developed an Ontario Committee on Government Productivity which was intended to free Deputy Ministers from policies so they could concentrate on programs. The Committee and its Policies and Priorities Board were abolished in the middle 1980s. But according to the 1987 text, the Quebec government was still operating on principles and a structure, similar to Ontario's former Policy and Priorities Board.[17]

Policies are not all of one sort of decision making. Political, policy decisions are different than bureaucratic policy decisions. And, quoting from the conclusion of a 1967 article about "Public Bureaucracy", "The official apparatus is often legalistic and bound up in red tape; yet much of this comes from the passion for accountability which the public brings to government. Here, perhaps, a change in the external environment is the main requirement for improvement".[18] Historical models of change, aren't always applicable though. For example 100% debt-to-GDP, Canada 1945 after War II, was reduced to 20% by 1974. But Canada's debt-to-GDP had risen again to 75% by 1995 when changes to the external environment couldn't be compared to environmental conditions of 1945 which didn't exist, because 1995 interest rates were high, and there wasn't massive military spending to be cut. The federal Finance Minister had to use other measures. What does GDP mean to Canada's Federal Finance Department? "GDP" and "debt-to-GDP ratio" are defined in the GLOSSARY OF TERMS. Debt-to-GDP ratio is an effective way to view federal deficits and debts. According to Finance Minister, Paul Martin, the ratio is a relationship between two variables. "Debt is about what we owe. GDP is about what we do." Viewed from the point of view of the federal debt, the ratio was rising relentlessly over two decades

1975 ratio was about 19%
1985 ratio was about 50%
1995 ratio was about 75%

Viewed from the point of view of budgetary deficits,

1993/94 debt to GDP ratio about 6% = $42 billion deficit
1994/95 ratio was about 5% = $37.5 billion deficit
1995/96 ratio was about 4.5% = $28.6 billion deficit
Subsequent ratios were lower than expected
1996/97 lower at $8.9 billion deficit
1997/98 lower than 2% debt-to-GDP ratio [19]

Here we're leading into questions about other historical tendencies of Canada'a debt. For example, the federal Department of Finance understands the ratio in terms of the federal debt, independent of provincial government debts and debts of municipalities. Debts by governments in Canada far exceed Gross Domestic Product, but we can't wander into those trends. Neither can we attend to issues about growth and about damaging effects on the environment caused by excessive industrial growth. Definitions of "performance norms", of and among government debts, and definitions of "Trends" are in the GLOSSARY OF TERMS.

In policies concerned with government programs, issues are impossible to summarize among almost infinite conditions of policy proposals, formulations and implementations among the many players of the public at large, interest groups, politicians and bureaucrats and the media. Policy decisions of the kinds Norman Cragg was involved, as a senior bureaucrat in the beginning of the Canada Assistance Plan, were sort of ex post facto, after the fact of the formulation of the legislation into the Act, Regulation and Agreements by the Government of Canada; and after many years of political policy making had transpired before the Canada Assistance Plan came into being. After CAP was established and provincial claims were made on the federal government, for funding programs in the provinces of Canada, policies were necessary to interpret federal legislation of the Act, Regulations and Agreements to the provinces. And in the provinces, Acts and Regulations were legislated, and policy making at political levels in each province was necessary before bureaucrats of the provinces could establish policies in coordination with the federal bureaucrats. Beyond these, it's impossible to summarize issues and policies among the many players of the public at large, interest groups, politicians and bureaucrats and the media.[20]

Digressing further about organizational metaphors, here's my review/report of a published article about present scenes from the electronic superhighways; an article from **FELICITOR**, September/October 1993 "Digitization: the New Preservation Medium?" by MacGregor Patterson. The writer was mainly concerned, in his composition of this article, with records preservation but his research included all sorts of significance about digitization, and about other electronic forms and techniques. It's not a global world but a compact, dynamic interactive inventory. Now, as though to allow much of the article to fade away, my review/report quotes the writer in condensed viewpoints of the inventory, as though in one continuing spaced quotation.

"Digitization offers the flexibility of scanning images and storing them in computer databases where they can be indexed and retrieved (perhaps by several users at once) in a manner far beyond the capabilities of micrographics. p. 22... Microfilm...microgaphics reprography medium is durable with a relatively long life span, offers savings in space, is inexpensive, involving a relatively uncomplicated process. ...if it were not for the emergence of digital imaging, the suitability of microfilm for reprography purposes might never be an issue... Computer storage media ...seem especially transitory...breakdown of organic resins... of magnetic tapes or discs makes them reliable for five to ten years only... CD ROM, the most common form of optical device...age at a...rapid rate...problem with optical discs...far less perfect world where they must work...though the EON DISC may have better archival capabilities than the CD ROM, it is not downwardly compatible ... computer technologies ... are hardware dependent The progress of computer memory media from punch card, to magnetic tape, to optical discs, has involved corresponding (and expensive) changes in the necessary equipment...Owners with eight-track tapes are well aware of the consequences of the loss of hardware support, as are institutions with data stored on computer punch cards. p. 23...combining the old technologies of punch cards and microfiche. Here the computer reads the index data from the card as the image is scanned from the film. Proponents of ...hybrid (micrographic-computer) systems see potential for growth in development of digital imaging..."

And so the article goes on through "non-metalic mylar memory"; barcode labels; CAD/COM; Mini Disc (MD)...has read- write capabilities; WORM ...downwardly incompatible; AIIM... products more suitable for potential users. "If new photo images are digitized pixels rather than chemically altered grains of silver nitrate, the question of computer storage versus mylar is reduced to which is the most cost effective storage media." "Evolutions in technology...an accepted part of the most modern work environments."..."the world is becoming digitally oriented." "SONY's new Discman Electronic Book Player...text and sound on a hand held computer." "plan now for the possibility of...being overwhelmed by the accelerating pace of technological change." pp. 23-26.

I wonder, not to be facetious, who should do the planning?
MacGregor Patterson's reply might refer the question to his bibliography, up to 1992, of over thirty bibliographical references on page 27[21]. (Also, see APPENDIX XIX "RECORDS MANAGEMENT AND INFORMATION TECHNOLOGY")

FOOTNOTES TO CHAPTER 4. "METAPHORS OF PUBLIC ADMINISTRATION"

1. THE Y.M.C.A. IN CANADA by Murray Ross, THE RYERSON PRESS, TORONTO, JUNE 1951, PART V CONCLUSION.

2. THE GREAT CODE, THE BIBLE AND LITERATURE, by Northrop Frye, published by the Penguin Group, Penguin Books of Canada Limited, 10 Alcorn Avenue, Toronto, Ontario, Canada, M4V 3B2; ISBN 0-14-012928-6 260 page 26.

3. DECADES OF SERVICE, A History of the Ontario Ministry of Community and Social Services, by Clifford Williams. Copyright, 1984 the Ministry of Community and Social Services; ISBN 0-7743-9004-2

4. THE GREAT CODE, THE BIBLE AND LITERATURE, by Northrop Frye, published by the Penguin Group, Penguin Books of Canada Limited, 10 Alcorn Avenue, Toronto, Ontario, Canada, M4V 3B2; ISBN 0-14-012928-6 260 pages, p.136.

5. Ibid p. xviii

6. Ibid p. 88

7. Ibid p. 190

8. Ibid p. 250 (See the GLOSSARY of TERMS re "Leviathan")

9. Ibid p. 49

10. Ibid p. 22

11. Ibid p. 11

12. Ibid p. 75

13. CANADIAN PUBLIC ADMINISTRATION, The Journal of the Institute of Public Administration of Canada, Winter 1994, Volume 37, Number 4.

14. PUBLIC ADMINISTRATION IN CANADA, SELECTED READINGS, edited by W.D.K. KERNAGHAN and A.M. WILLMS, published by Methuen Publications, Toronto 1971."The Management Theory Jungle Revisited" by Donald Austin Woolf p. 20, (footnote #4 in the article).

15. CANADIAN PUBLIC ADMINISTRATION, The Journal of the Institute of Public Administration of Canada, Fall 1989, Volume 32, Number 3. pp. 382-406. "Member's Survey on theory, practice and innovation in public administration", by James Iain Gow, p. 391.

16. PUBLIC ADMINISTRATION IN CANADA, SELECTED READINGS, edited by W.D.K. KERNAGHAN and A.M. WILLMS,

17. PUBLIC ADMINISTRATION IN CANADA, A TEXT, Second Edition by Kenneth Kernaghan and David Siegel, published by Methuen Publications, Toronto 1987, 642 pages, 1987 ISBN 0-458-80650-1.

18. PUBLIC ADMINISTRATION IN CANADA, SELECTED READINGS, edited by W.D.K.

KERNAGHAN and A.M. WILLMS, quotation from p. 331 re PUBLIC ADMINISTRATION, "The Bureaucracy", by J.W.Pfiffner and R.V. Presthus, published by Ronald Press, New York, 1967.

19. Budget Data, 1995 to 1997 and data from speeches to the Finance Committee, supplied by The Honourable Paul Martin, Minister of Finance, Government of Canada.

20. THE WELFARE, A Concise Archival History of Social Services, quoted "A Speech by Norman A. Cragg" in APPENDIX I, edited and published by Kenneth Coward, printed by Stan Brown Printers, Owen Sound 1994. Also, the speech is reprinted here in the "PREFACE".

21. **"Digitization: The New Preservation Medium?"** by MacGregor Patterson, published by the Canadian Library Association's magazine, **FELICITOR,** September/October 1993.

CHAPTER 5
MEDIA IN CANADA

PERIODICALS AS MEDIA

Menus for information in Canada nowadays provide infinite, well organized sources and angles of editing information as compared with information sources before government became extensively involved in complex social organizations. Periodicals, referred to in the FOOTNOTES of APPENDIX XVIII, indicate only a few organized sources and angles of editing information directly or indirectly, in advocating health and welfare interests throughout early history of periodicals. Two of the advocative periodicals, titled SOCIAL WELFARE and CANADIAN MAGAZINE, reported on health and welfare news early in the 20th century, and their titles were included in later published indexes of Canadian Periodicals. In 1965, articles about the "Canada Assistance Plan" were published in a periodical, CANADIAN WELFARE, #s 41:105 & 41:138, My-Je.'65. And an article about "War on Poverty" (Canada Assistance Plan) was published in the LABOUR GAZETTE #65:794-8, S'65, not an advocative periodical per se. The 1965 articles were also included among indexes of Canadian Periodicals.[1]

Professional Journals, and other sorts of periodicals, which specialize in articles about health and welfare, are more advocative than are popular periodicals. But most journals specializing in articles about health and welfare, such as Medical Journals and Canadian Psychology aren't recorded in indexes of Canadian Periodicals like those listed in Footnotes of APPENDIX XVIII. But periodicals such as the following are included in the CANADIAN INDEX TO PERIODICALS 1985, Canadian Banker, Canadian Architects, Canadian Journal of Education, Canadian Historical Association, Canadian Journal of Criminology, Canadian Journal of Political and Social Theories, Canadian Journal of Political Science, Canadian Mental Health, Canadian Review of Sociology and Anthropology, and a Quebec periodical "Protect Yourself" for Consummateur. I've not reviewed professional periodicals here. Most earlier professional journals were published in the U.S.A., and even today, almost all professional academic journals, such as about sociology, and about psychology, continue to be about sociology and psychology in the U.S.A. Needless to say, all sorts of errors about health and welfare in Canada are inspired by information in professional journals from the U.S.A.. Not to say the errors are all errors of commissions; most are errors of omissions.

Not errors of omissions in the U.S.A. but omissions in Canada. Writings about the U.S.A. in periodicals in the U.S.A., by American sociologists and psychologists, aren't writings about Canada. However, and in contradiction to my above comments about articles in American periodicals, some articles by Canadians appear in American periodicals; all sorts of questions would need to be answered about each such article before any Canadian significance could be commented upon about such articles.

Some readers of this study of history might be distracted when I beg off some issues, concerns and questions. I acknowledge that many decision-makers eagerly seek information and hard facts on subjects which are discussed here; however the present study is A HISTORY OF THE CANADA ASSISTANCE PLAN. The study isn't An Outline of History, and it certainly isn't THE History of the Canada Assistance Plan. For issues, concerns and questions, take for examples Day Care for Children. Should decision makers side with private or public Day Care? subsidized or unsubsidized? At what ages? Are there differences between "concerns" and "issues"? And there are many other questions generated by such questions which this study couldn't possibly attempt to sort out.

What sort of news obtains space in magazines, and on radio and TV broadcasts, in nations where inflation is raging? In such nations, news predominantly features current trends of money values. Canada, in 1997 - 1998, became involved with deflation as the value of the Canadian dollar began to girate around a value of 70 cents, falling to a value of approx. 63.0 cents, its lowest value ever vis-a-vis the U.S. dollar. Deflation got extra daily attention in the media. Before TV, and other sources of documentary news, newspapers used to bring out EXTRAS of editions which were usually sold on street corners on days the extra news occurred, usually on news about war. "EXTRA EXTRA, READ ALL ABOUT IT".

Not to intrude on possible theses but to elaborate and integrate Frye's knowledge into the scene of periodical literature, and into history, I discovered that "causality", i.e. causes and effects, according to Frye's interests, are mainly fictional. But in referring to fiction blended with sociology by an author named Zola, Frye provides an example of how fiction affects thinking.[2] "The sociological aspect by definition is a more direct rendering of "truth" than the fictional one". In APPENDIX XVIII I've attempted to reason historically with data about poetry from Indexes of Canadian Periodicals. Most fictional renderings of "cause" aren't pertinent to a history of THE CANADA ASSISTANCE PLAN, except that persons who create the data of the history live and think within a mix of history, languages, rhetoric, emotions and metaphors which play upon causes of decision-making.

MACLEAN'S MAGAZINE AS MEDIA

In early history of MACLEAN'S, some articles about health and welfare of Canadians did appear; amidst columns of entertainment in Maclean's, including short stories until recent years. Later articles about health and welfare continued to appear among articles and items of news information. In early and later years, some journalists of Maclean's specialized in advocative articles about health and welfare. E.C. Drury, a 1920's Premier of Ontario, who encouraged and supported Welfare legislation for Ontario in the 1920s, was an early advocative contributor to Maclean's. Later contributors of articles were Sidney Katz and June Callwood, both of whom specialized in articles about health and welfare. Periodicals which specialized in advocacy articles probably influenced writers like Sydney Katz and June Callwood.

In the 1920s, 1930s and 1940s, Maclean's didn't handle news as thoroughly as Maclean's handles news nowadays, but I wouldn't want to judge which articles have more merit, those from bygone years or those of today. No matter how thorough and detailed are items and articles of news, journalism can't report all the news. Maclean's published many articles about Child Welfare in the 1920s, and periodicals, such as SOCIAL WELFARE, regularly carried news about social services, although there wasn't nearly as much social service in the earlier and middle decades of the twentieth century. When welfare programs were established in the 1920s, government expenditures on social services were infinitely lower, as noted in DECADES OF SERVICE by Clifford J. Williams[3], and in THE WELFARE by Kenneth Coward[4].

I've done some research about articles and items appearing in Maclean's news at specified intervals of the 1990s. How should an article be defined? How should an item be defined? Neither articles nor items are "news" only of course, but I've made no attempt to explain differences of what is "news" and what isn't. And quotation marks I'm using aren't intended in any way to reflect on the integrity of items and articles in Maclean's. Is research of "news" like research of myths in literature, movies, live theatre or operas, or any other art form? Does "news" concentrate on "good" or "evil" to report that "evil" prevails or that "good" prevails. Should I suggest that "news", like myths, profits from "evil", and from "good" of course. "Evil" and "good" mean all sorts of things to all sorts of people. Northrop Frye attends to this sort of variety of meanings, distinguishing dictionary or conventional definitions from meaning in what we "read" for example, but not especially about "evil" nor "good". Frye quoted Carl Sanburg,

The fog comes
On little cat feet [5]

In this study of history of THE CANADA ASSISTANCE PLAN, "evil" and "good" shouldn't be a concentration of the study even if we're involved with sorting out dictionary or conventional meanings versus everyday usages. And research rationales sorting out "news" in Maclean's shouldn't involve much concentration on "evil" and "good" for purposes of relating periodicals to social services. How then should news items and articles be researched?

According to Maclean's, "What Matters to Canadians" is what is published. So there's a broad scope for sorting published reports in research about social services. I was going to use the word "anomie" within a classification of articles, for atypical cross references of the research as needed, as would research of "good" and "evil" be cross referenced atypically. Not to be facetious, nor to overburden the research, "anomie" is a condition of normlessness, and it's unlikely MACLEAN'S is ever normless, although the magazine publishes articles which could be classified as amidst conditions of "anomie". Most such articles aren't pertinent to a history of THE CANADA ASSISTANCE PLAN.

CARP PUBLICATION AS MEDIA

CARP News, The Canadian Association for Retired Persons, a national, independent publication for 50-plus lifestyles, is published every other month; members and subscribers receive their copies by mail. In December 1998, Volume 14, Number 6 was published. The editorials of CARP tend to be aggressive, advocating on behalf of pensioners on many fronts. Articles and advertisements cover many subjects of advice. Issues faced by most "persons in need" and "persons likely to be in need", unless they are seniors, aren't within the scope of CARP.

CARP didn't cover issues and concerns of CAP, because The Canada Assistance Plan included assistance, benefits and welfare services to all ages of "persons in need" and "persons likely to be in need". But existing social services, which were previously funded under the Canada Assistance Plan, and continuing social security agencies, are interested in the advocative approach of CARP. Whence this History of the Canada Assistance Plan reviews purposes and entanglements of the advocative field. It's a difficult field to review where all sorts of sentiments and emotions are positioned. And irresolutions, not the least of which are in issues of accountabilities, are on all sides of the advocative field. How can advocates be accountable? Most aggressions of advocates are aimed at governments where accountability is supposed to be among politicians and bureaucrats. But, if advocative purposes are achieved, after advocates aggressively lobbied governments, have the advocates been accountable? These questions cannot be answered in this context. Indeed, are the above questions in proper order?

Nevertheless, whether or not the questions are in proper order, the questions exist among advocates, among decision makers of governments, among persons who benefit from favourable decisions, among persons who don't benefit, and among the population at large. All these players put the questions in many different ways of course. And in such a complicated advocative culture, many of the questions aren't stated interrogatively. According to THE GREAT CODE, by Northrop Frye, languages developed in ancient and less ancient cultural conditions, and modern languages also developed and continue to develop in cultural conditions.[6] So, assuming we're observing cultural conditions, among many players on all sides of the advocative field, it probably isn't unusual for language to be expressed in unusual ways, such as questions not being stated interrogatively.

THE BIBLE AS MEDIA

A History of THE CANADA ASSISTANCE PLAN shouldn't imply any sort of direct connections between the Bible and social services, even though there are many religious organizations which provide social services. Some religious organizations which provide social services don't follow the teachings of the Bible however. So this section about Biblical media doesn't intend in any way to proselytize about the Bible, nor about, nor for, any religious organization. I defer almost totally, to the scholarly teachings of Northrop Frye and his study in THE GREAT CODE. And, I defer to Frye as he refers to many other religions, in many parts of his study. The Bible in English, beginning from earliest translation, made from the original Latin and Greek, created an uproar and its author was executed in 1536. Since then, it has been composed in several versions. The King James Version was published in 1611, revised 1881-1885. Thereafter, the American Standard Version was published in 1901, and further revisions were made in 1952.[7] Many other earlier Versions of the Bible included Old Testament, Hebrew Scriptures. And, the Roman Catholic Latin Vulgate from the 6th century was used for English translations of the New Testament in 1582 and the Old Testament in 1609. The history of the Bible in England extends back to Early English, Anglo Saxon translations from Latin, from the 7th century onward.[8] Northrop Frye uses the AV, i.e."the Authorized Version of 1611" for quotations.[9] When I quote from Frye on any subject, I do so directly from his book THE GREAT CODE. Sometimes, while following Frye's "Index of Passages", from the Bible, when I look for passages in the 1952 Revised Standard Version, I discover differences betweeen the 1611 Version and the 1952 Version. Differences aren't significant here, because we're not involved with biblical criticism. But I've wondered whether or not, rather than the Bible, I should have used NORTHROP FRYE ON SHAKESPEARE, and/or some of Frye's other writings, for concepts to enlighten A History of the Canada Assistance Plan. For example, Frye noted that Shakespeare used plays within plays in many dramas, and I believe plays within plays exist in the Bible. Plays and dreams are universally experienced, so whether or not one or the other should have precedence is a matter of choice or judgement. But, I think a dream within a dream, or dreams within dreams, rather than a play, or plays within a play, is nearer to the pertinence of the Bible for enlightenment of A History of the Canada Assistance Plan. Shakespeare used the play within a play for A MIDSUMMER NIGHT'S DREAM, whence the playwright made the dream secondary to the play. Howsoever, I've used THE GREAT CODE by Frye, instead of NORTHROP FRYE ON SHAKESPEARE.

Books of the Bible, namely NUMBERS of the Old Testament, and REVELATION of the New Testament, were selected here, as I followed Northrop Frye's "Index of Passages", because they seem to historically represent the Old Testament and the New Testament. The BOOK of NUMBERS with its functions of numbers, is also significant, because the study of A History of The Canada Assistance Plan is deeply involved with numbers. The apocalyptic functions of the BOOK of REVELATION is significant, because the Bible inclines to be apocalyptic. (See my review of the Bible's BOOK OF REVELATIONS here below). Government expenditures inclined to be apocalyptic during the latter years of existence of the Canada Assistance Plan, but not especially because of the Canada Assistance Plan. (See the GLOSSARY OF TERMS for my definition of "Apocalypse".)

Before going into biblical inspirations, I must emphasize that we're here involved with A History of the Canada Assistance Plan. The Plan's original inspirations included the following quote from the speech by Norman Cragg,"In his statement on the Canada Assistance Plan made in the House on April 6th, 1965, the Prime Minister referred particularly to the wide support for a comprehensive program of public assistance that had been expressed by welfare organizations and authorities including the Canada Welfare Council." (the complete speech is in the PREFACE here) Some people might recall that the President of the U.S.A., at the time, referred to the American inspiration as a "War on Poverty". But the fact that war was the background inspiration of the Book of NUMBERS, reviewed here from the Bible, isn't intended to mix up metaphors in this history of the Canada Assistance Plan. Music of and by young people nowadays might call this sort of thinking hip hop.

As my narrative immediately follows here, where I directly recall the Bible for context, no footnotes are used for my comments, whether or not I refer to scriptures of the Bible. Moses and Aaron needed to bring order among the tribes of Israel, to prepare for war, so they organized a census of all the tribes. It's much more efficient to regiment numbers than it is to regiment words, hence the ordering of the tribes of Israel by census numbers, according to population cohorts, mainly male. The Book of NUMBERS is a record of the census and of bringing order among the tribes of Israel. Readers are welcome to disagree with me about biblical narration as to whether or not the Bible's more dreamlike than like plays within plays, especially when reading NUMBERS, because there certainly are all sorts of themes digressing from the intended control of the people. Frye's observations about the Books of Moses, are different than my elaborations of the Book of NUMBERS. Frye didn't observe controls of numerical aspects in language, but here's an example of similar effect in Frye's analysis of language, "God gives detailed instructions for constructing the ark of the covenant and similar sacred objects, and a craftsman named Bezaleel is appointed for the task. In ordinary written prose we should expect one sentence saying that Bezaleel made all these things as he was commanded to do. (Exedus 25ff) We actually get, in Exedus 36ff., a repetition of each detail, with "and thou shalt make" transposed to "and he made". Such repetition is primarily to impress the reader with the importance of what is being done, but the conventions are closer to those of oral literature."[10]

Here again no footnotes are used for my text as I've developed other sorts of context as well as biblical. With numerical records of, as in the study of expenditures of governments, a whole page of data immediately impresses readers with a single concept. For examples, columns of data in CHAPTER 2 which illustrate immediately each concept of each column's title, whereas to explain the same concepts with words would need many many words, repetitiously. Notwithstanding, in Old Testament times, pages of biblical narration were ongoing without breaks between words and without stanzas or verses. Of course, 4000 years, or so, ago in the times of Moses and Aaron, pages of numbers, or of words, weren't readily available, and most people couldn't comprehend them anyway. It's likely that neither could most of the commanders comprehend the census numbers, so the emphasis on commands over the people of Israel would need to be maintained by the top command where pages of numbers, and of narration, were comprehended. Ironically, nowadays, neither are coded numbers, stored in data processing memories, understandable at all times, nor always readily available on pages as the numbers accumulate in data processing technology. For now though, lets try following the processing of NUMBERS and REVELATION from the Bible. By the way, the following simplified outlines won't satisfy researchers who are led afar from outlines when they are reading referenced biblical text. But footnotes used by scholars of the Revised Standard Version, yield the following data information:

NUMBERS in the Old Testament

7 Old Testament books were footnoted, and
7 New Testament books were footnoted.

The New Testament didn't exist when NUMBERS was written. Neither were many of the Old Testament books yet written when NUMBERS was composed. And other earlier sources weren't noted nor footnoted. Topics from the 4 other Books of Moses were footnoted in NUMBERS, presumably brought to NUMBERS from the others, except DEUTERONOMY as a sequal to NUMBERS.

2 from GENESIS
16 from EXEDUS
13 from LEVITICUS
13 to DEUTERONOMY

Other footnotes in NUMBERS, regarding Old Testament Books, were presumably topics taken, 1 to PSALMS, 1 to CHRONICLES and 3 to JOSHUA from NUMBERS. NUMBERS itself was footnoted 24 times, referencing chapters and verses of the Book of NUMBERS itself. Books of the New Testament footnoted in NUMBERS, for topics taken, included

1 for LUKE,
3 for ACTS,
2 for 1 CORINTHIANS,
4 for HEBREWS,
1 for TIMOTHY,
1 for MATTHEW and
1 for REVELATION.

REVELATION in the New Testament

21 Old Testament books were footnoted, and
7 New Testament books were footnoted.

REVELATION is the last book of the Bible, so all footnotes refer to topics brought to the Book of Revelation by John, from the Old and New Testaments, and from other sources. Except 5 topics footnoted from REVELATION itself. From the Books of Moses, (i.e. from first 5 Old Testament books) to REVELATION footnotes included

9 from GENESIS
22 from EXEDUS
2 from LEVITICUS
2 from NUMBERS
5 from DEUTERONOMY

Other Old Testament books, referenced in REVELATIONS, with topics footnoted are

48 from ISAIAH
32 from EZEKIEL
28 from DANIEL
28 from PSALMS
20 from JEREMIAH
11 from KINGS
10 from ZECHARIAH
8 from JOEL
3 from HOSEA
2 from JOB
2 from PROVERBS
1 from MALACHI
1 from AMOS

New Testament books, referenced in REVELATIONS, with topics footnoted are

3 from MATTHEW
2 from MARK
1 from LUKE
1 from JOHN
1 from ACTS
1 from 1 THESSALONIANS
1 from 2 THESSALONIANS [11]

According to Northrop Frye, "Anyone coming 'cold' to the Book of Revelation, without context of any kind, would probably regard it as simply an insane rhapsody. It has been described as a book that either finds a man mad or else leaves him so. And yet, if we were to explore below the repressions in our own minds that keep us 'normal,' we might find very similar nightmares of anxiety and triumph. As a parallel example, we may cite the so-called Tibetan Book of the Dead, where the soul is assumed immediately after death to be going through a series of visions, first of peaceful and then of wrathful dieties. A priest reads the book into the ear of the corpse, who is also assumed to hear the readers voice telling him that all these visions are simply his own repressed mental forms now released by death and coming to the surface. If he could realize that, he would immediately be delivered from their power, because it is his own power."[12]

In our everyday modern world of effort, work and struggle, above the "repressions in our own minds" we might find, in writings and speech, about the "Protestant ethic", or of the "moral economy", advice which keeps in our consciousness some of our fears which we might otherwise take to our nightmares. (see the Glossary of Terms for definitions of "Protestant ethic" and "moral economy".)

FOOTNOTES OF CHAPTER 5: MEDIA IN CANADA

1. CANADIAN INDEX TO PERIODICALS, 1960, edited by Isabel Bradley, Lenore Aedly, Sheila Egoff, Ottawa, published by the Canadian Library Association, p.366.

2. THE GREAT CODE, THE BIBLE AND LITERATURE, by Northrop Frye, published by the Penguin Group, Penguin Books of Canada Limited, 10 Alcorn Avenue, Toronto, Ontario, Canada, M4V 3B2; ISBN 0-14-012928-6 260 pages, p.25.

3. DECADES OF SERVICE, A History of the Ontario Ministry of Community and Social Services, by Clifford Williams. Copyright, 1984 the Ministry of Community and Social Services; ISBN 0-7743-9004-2, Chapters 1 to 5

4. THE WELFARE, A Concise Archival History of Social Services, by Kenneth Coward, printed by Stan Brown Printers Limited, Owen Sound, Ontario; ISBN 0-9698635-0-0, p. 1.

5. THE GREAT CODE, THE BIBLE AND LITERATURE, by Northrop Frye, pp.57-58.

6. THE GREAT CODE, THE BIBLE AND LITERATURE, by Northrop Frye, pp. 3-30, and 199-233.

7. **THE HOLY BIBLE, CONTAINING THE OLD AND NEW TESTAMENTS,** Revised Standard Version, Thomas Nelson and Sons, Toronto. Old Testament Section Copyright 1952, New Testament Section Copyright 1946. Copyrights by Division of Christian Education of the National Council of the Churches of Christ in the United States of America. "PREFACE".

8. **THE HOLY BIBLE, CONTAINING THE OLD AND NEW TESTAMENTS,** Revised Standard Version, "BIBLE STUDY HELPS", pp.4-7 (at the back of the Bible).

9. THE GREAT CODE, THE BIBLE AND LITERATURE, by Northrop Frye, p.xiii

10. Ibid p.214.

11. **THE HOLY BIBLE,** CONTAINING THE OLD AND NEW TESTAMENTS, Revised Standard Version. Books NUMBERS and REVELATIONS.

12. THE GREAT CODE, THE BIBLE AND LITERATURE, by Northrop Frye, p.137.

CONCLUSION

The historical theme of this study, of THE CANADA ASSISTANCE PLAN, didn't aim for conclusions, but information included in the study and in working papers of the study, and other sources of information not elaborated in the study, do lead to conclusions. In the text, I've referred to and repeated a comment of mine from Chapter 4 and Appendices I & XIII, "It's a good thing we have Acts, Regulations and Policies as functioning organizations terminate." The social services organizations which terminated during the years of the Canada Assistance Plan, especially toward and after 1996, were mostly agencies which depended on subsidies from provincial governments; and, under cost sharing arrangements provincial governments depended on funding from the federal government. I conclude that most organizations which terminated through the history of THE CANADA ASSISTANCE PLAN, 1966 to 1996, were casualties in conditions of exceptional budgetary expenditures, not necessarily government spending on programs of the Canada Assistance Plan. Facing massive debts of year-by-year deficits which were adding up to more debt each year in Canada, the federal government had to control and govern expenditures. Obviously it was decided, CAP's open ended programs were to be controlled. Examples of federal funding cut-backs from 1990 to 1996 can be seen in the Restraints Act; for governments with the highest revenues and expenditures - Ontario, Alberta and British Columbia - Federal Contributions were restrained from increasing beyond an annual growth 5% higher above the federal contributions made over the 1989-90 base year.

When the Canada Assistance Plan ended, Canada's provinces continued to provide for persons in need under provincial legislations, and the federal government established funding arrangements under Canada's Health and Social Contract. These arrangements however, aren't open-ended; the result is provincial funding short-falls for many agencies. And Health's insatiable appetite for more and more funding is bound to need more and more out of the Social Contract.

Role-playing and dreams are universally common phenomena in experiences and behaviours of men and women. But information isn't universally available for the roles and dreams of experiences and behaviours, no more nor less so in public administration than in everyday lives of Canadians affected by public administration. And available information, like plays within plays, or dreams within dreams, is constantly in flux. This historical study attempts to present significant records of data and conceptual information. Data here presented can be verified by tracking the footnotes and bibliographies, but infinite concepts in public and private affairs can never be tracked, except as reported, and except in the forms of reporting. At the end of 1998 and early in 1999, many news reports referred to negotiations between the provincial governments and the federal government about proposals for a "SOCIAL UNION". The news reports about negotiations illustrate an unacknowledged conflict between reports which will surely develop SOCIAL CONFLICT in a distracted "SOCIAL UNION". Some reports include statements which imply that the SOCIAL UNION should or will demand that never again will the federal government withdraw funding from the provinces for established programs. While in retrospect about recent times when funding was withdrawn from the provinces, the demand then was that the federal government must never again incur deficits or debts which would cause conditions where funding would have to be withdrawn. These two contradictory demands will lead to SOCIAL CONFLICT. (See "Conflict" defined in the GLOSSARY)

Furthermore, about the "SOCIAL UNION", its intiatives appear different than the original inspirations of the Canada Assistance Plan. For more information via the internet, the Social Union website address is http://socialunion.gc.ca. To quote: "This website provides an overview of activities associated with the social union." Northrop Frye's writings elaborate about apocalypse, but he admits to "overspiced stew" of his writings.[1] He also elaborates about wandering imperfections.[2] Would that I could transcribe the context of his words to complexes here of my context. However the APPENDICES following here are more pertinent to A HISTORY OF THE CANADA ASSISTANCE PLAN.

Many varying conditions lead a history to curiosities about human destinies. In nature, during late August in south-western Ontario, bird watchers, and other casual observers of flora and fauna, are very much aware of impending months of fall and winter. Tiny and small birds, such as humming-birds and wrens, are still here but sensing approaching times for migration, as a restless person in bed might be aware of the clock and an approaching hour whence to rise from the bed to attend an important appointment. The Canada Assistance Plan provided a similar sense of time-keeping for many people during the 30 years of its existence, but the legislation was surely never intended as a final destiny for anyone. And personnel of public administration in direct or indirect work of social services through most of the history of THE CANADA ASSISTANCE PLAN never thought it would eventually terminate.

1.   THE GREAT CODE, THE BIBLE AND LITERATURE, by Northrop Frye, published by the Penguin Group, Penguin Books of Canada Limited, 10 Alcorn Avenue, Toronto, Ontario, Canada, M4V 3B2; ISBN 0-14-012928-6 260 pages. p.15

2.   Ibid p.168

GLOSSARY OF TERMS

Terms amplified by this glossary are significant to a study of A HISTORY OF THE CANADA ASSISTANCE PLAN, although some of the terms aren't in the text of the study. Most of the terms are included in dictionaries and thesauruses and used by texts and other published material in many different usages.

Accumulated Deficit:
(see Deficit)

Actuals:
Financial records usually distinguish recorded expenditures and revenues with the term "actuals", distinguished from the term "estimates". (See below definition of "estimates".)

Advocates:
Persons, speaking, writing or acting on behalf of concerns shared with other persons. Persons also speak, write or act on behalf of issues. Concerns and issues aren't always defined in the same way.

Apocalypse:
The definition of this word is widely understood to refer to cataclysm in natural and social conditions. Some people believe that an apocalypse is inevitable; teachings of such people are referred to as apocalyptic. Extreme apocalyptic teachings include beliefs that only true believers will be saved in the apocalypse. The Bible's Book of Revelations is apocalyptic. See THE GREAT CODE by Northrop Frye.[1]

Assistance:
The General Welfare Assistance Act of Ontario is an act of social services, but it's unlike the Welfare Services Act. (See "Welfare" and "Welfare Services"). In Metropolitan Toronto, for example, the original Department known as the Welfare Department became the Department of Social Services, and subsequently became the Department of Community and Social Services. Financial reports of Metro Toronto use the term Social and Family Services to refer to expenditures of social services' programs. Many expenditures for programs of Metro such as Housing, Homes for the Aged, and Nursing Homes weren't shareable under the Canada Assistance Plan. Assistance of Social Services is provided in assistance payments, in supplementary aid and in special assistance to persons in need. Also, Assistance of Social Services include Homes of Special Care, Child Welfare and other programs. Expenditures for "assistance" are under the General Welfare Assistance Act and Regulations in Ontario, and under other Acts with Regulations such as Child Welfare. For information about Ontario's "assistance" payments, see Ontario's Acts and Regulations; or, for information about "assistance" in other provinces, see their similar legislation. Details of expenditures of all the provinces and territories of Canada are outlined in federal catalogues of SOCIAL SECURITY STATISTICS.[2] For more definitive terms and reports, applicable to the Canada Assistance Plan, see Canada Assistance Plan, Annual Report(s).[3]

Calendar years:
Years ending 31 December are usually "Calendar years", as in censuses by Statistics Canada.

Concern:
Feelings of concern, felt about many conditions and events, are usually happy or worried feelings among persons. Senses of identity usually accompany feelings of concern, felt greater by nearer proximities, and/or relationships and by former and/or continuing conditions and events.

Conflict:
The word "conflict", used in this study refers to disagreements or prejudices which might be conscious or unconscious, personal or social, but uses of the word don't include violence. The word "conflict" can be used in all sorts of contexts, and it therefore begs all sorts of questions which are unattended in this study. To my knowledge, "conflict theory" isn't attended in theories of Public Administration in Canada. Such theories could be used with regard to conflicting news reports pertinent to the "SOCIAL UNION" which emerged in federal-provincial relations during the years after the end of the Canada Assistance Plan. (See my "CONCLUSIONS" in this study of "A HISTORY..")

Consultation:
On matters of concern, and on matters of issues, persons consult with each other. Consultants may or may not be directly involved with matters which have been or which will be subjects of decision making. (see "Lobbyists").

Contrive:
Conscious persistent efforts to control an event or events; or "contrived" control of an event or events.

Debt: See "Public Debt" and "Debt to GDP ratio"..

Debt-to-GDP-ratio:
The term is often referenced by Canada's Finance Minister to explain several conditions of federal budgets, referring to government debt in relation to Gross Domestic Product (what Canada produces). Catalogues of SOCIAL SECURITY STATISTICS, by Human Resources Canada, reference "GDP" in other ways without reference to "debt". See Table 1, and see the Appendices of the catalogues. Actually, "debt" reference to "GDP" should be plural, as "debts-to-GDP-ratio" to refer to all debts of all governments in Canada; federal budgets only indirectly reference provincial budgets.

Deficit:
Differences between revenues and expenditures, each year, indicate the amounts of deficits each year when expenditures exceed revenues. "Accumulated deficits at the end of the year", each year, are amounts taken forward to each following year as "Accumulated deficits at beginning of the year", each year.

Deficits:
Accumulated deficits are, in effect, the debt, usually reported as "Accumulated deficit - beginning of the year" and "Accumulated deficit - end of the year". See APPENDIX VIII FINANCIAL DATA, PUBLIC ACCOUNTS OF CANADA.

Destiny:
Dictionaries associate the word, "destiny" with destination. Sects and some religions, and some Christian denominations, identify the word with predetermination. The many intervening variables in the uses of the word can't be attended in this history of The Canada Assistance Plan.

Dreams:
See "Protestant Ethic" and "Moral Economy"

Equalibrium:
All texts about the study of Economics describe equalibrium as variable conditions of "aggregate demand". There are also other conditions of equalibrium. (See "Stabilization")

Estimates:
Financial records as "estimates" are usually preliminary to records as "actuals". Estimates might be used at budget times to get on with the budget rather than wait for the actuals of spending times. "Estimates" might also be used in place of "actuals" when agreements are awaited between a supplier and a purchaser. The term "estimates" rather than "actuals" is also used in other circumstances. And there's always the possibility of misinterpretations of the uses of the terms "estimates" and "actuals", not always necessarily in references to records as alluded to here above. (See definition of "Actuals"). (See definition of "Mill Rates").In 1996, Metro Toronto received an award for budgetary presentations from "The Government Officers Finance Association of the United States and Canada... for Distinguished Budget Presentation to the Municipality of Metropolitan Toronto, Ontario for its annual budget for the fiscal year beginning January 1, 1996. In order to receive this award, a government unit must publish a budget document that meets program criteria as a policy document, as an operations guide, as a financial plan, and as a communication device."[4] A similar award was presented to Metro Toronto for 1995.

Exorcism:
Hocus-pocus by otherwise reasoning persons. (see "Ridicule")

Fiscal year:
All expenditure records of municipalities, provinces and the federal government ended their fiscal years, to do with the Canada Assistance Plan, each 31 March. Ancillary arrangements and agreements were adjusted to fiscal years accordingly. For example, Provincially Approved Agencies operating by calendar years adjusted to the fiscal year accounting of the municipalities and the provincial government.

Gross Domestic Product: (GDP)
This is a term used by economists. Canada's Minister of Finance often refers to the GDP as Canada's national product of goods and services expressed in billions of dollars. (See "debt-to-GDP ratio".)

Inflation:
All texts about the study of Economics describe inflation as variable conditions of "aggregate demand". There are also other conditions of inflation, but my references are to variables of aggregate demand. Conditions of inflation are undesireable for most persons. (See "Stabilization")

Issues:
Issues exist in circus-like operas of modern urban society. Agendas on some issues are hidden, or not apparent. (See "Lobbyists" and "Concerns").

Leviathan:
THE GREAT CODE, THE BIBLE & LITERATURE by Northrop Frye referenced monsters in a sort of Sunday School way about Leviathan, Behemoth and Dragon whereby the monsters get a bad objective rap so to speak. Not all cultures view(ed) "dragons" as evil monsters. Some cultures view(ed) "dragons" as more evil than do bible stories, not objectively, but rather in reaction formations. See Edmund Spenser's dragon in the poem, "Faerie Queen" and "NOTES" of the poem in REPRESENTATIVE POETRY, University of Toronto Press, 1958.

Lobbyists:
Persuasion is the function of a lobbyist. The role of a lobbyist is usually played out behind the scenes of issues which are openly known to decision makers and to persons who are affected by the decisions. Some lobbyists, intending to reinforce persuasions of decision makers, persuade opinions of persons who will be affected by decision makers. (See "Persuasion").

Microeconomics and Macroeconomics
These terms are found in all texts of ECONOMICS. The terms refer to economic theory and to governmental policies about economic activities.

Mill rates
"Mill rates" are established according to assessments, taxes and needed revenues for expenditures. The term "mill rates" was referenced so often in budgetary proceedings, in earlier years, it became a sort of metaphoric short hand. (See definition of "Estimates")

Moral economy
The term is a more recent reference than the term Protestant ethic, regarding attitudes toward work and the rewards of work. I've not read any writings on the subject. I've heard the term stated by concerned community leaders. Assuming the term to be contrary to dreamlike "Protestant ethics", inspirations of the concept "moral economy" might be charity, restraint, and role playing, involving behaviorism, and physical and mental exercises.

Notwithstanding
Dictionaries define the word as expressing "in spite of", but I usually intend to say, "not to neglect the fact that". Often, word meanings aren't obvious except by their context as with "notwithstanding", if undefined except by context.

Performance norms:
This term is used by sociologists. Performance norms in Canada are North American, although the global market place affects all sorts of normative behaviours. According to some sociologists, paramount performance norms in North America are achievement and maintenance. These, and other norms, aren't in conflict with each other, but people and organizations sometimes conflict with each other.

Persuasion:
Some manners of persuasion are overt. Some persuasions are subliminal. All persuasions ramify cultural structures.

Protestant ethic:
Hypothetical writings on the subject incline to polemics which suggest that the Protestant ethic drives economics in North America. Corollaries to the writings are the "American Dream", growth, work ethics, profit motives, maximized profits, inspirations and efforts. See "Moral economy" for a definition of a contrary hypotheses to the Protestant ethic.

Public Debt:
The term, "Public Debt" is used differently, historically, in records of Public Accounts. Debt may be owed to creditors by the federal government, or by provincial governments.

Public Debt Charges:
These charges affect calculations of expenditures, each year, and shortfalls between revenues and expenditures are referred to as deficits.

Rancor:
Some conditions meet with anger or more severe reactions in communities. A History of the Canada Assistance Plan can't illustrate the many conditions of rancor.

Reason:
True facts are required in the manners of reason. In this history of THE CANADA ASSISTANCE PLAN, true facts are mainly observable and verifiable. Necessities of reason are different than necessities of rhetoric. Untrue facts aren't true.

Record keeping:
It's impossible to define record keeping in a few words, because there are so many different functions and management methods. This history mainly refers to records of and by governments, especially regarding expenditures.

Rhetoric:
Rhetorical manners don't require true facts. Rhetorical necessities aren't required in this history of THE CANADA ASSISTANCE PLAN, but they're used, however; for examples, whenever the history begs off begged questions. Deliberate, deceptive uses of rhetorics involve untruths. All sorts of deliberate usages of untrue rhetorics can't be defined here.

Ridicule:
Definitions most often imply derision, insult, disrespect, but some people see persuasive possibilities in ridicule. Ridicule as persuasion is likely ironic satire. (see "Exorcism")

Role Playing:
See "Moral Economy" and "Protestant Ethic"

Social change:
The usage here is intended to be consistent with the usage of the term in humanities and social studies, referring to social changes in community organizations, environmental changes of all sorts, and social changes arising from phenomena. Social change in Canada isn't necessarily the same as social change in the U.S.A., nor is social change in Canada the same as social change anywhere else in the world.

Social Services:
The definition here refers to the way the word "services" appears in public use, including "assistance" of Social Services, but in Acts and Regulations, "welfare services" are different than usages in reference to "assistance" (see Ontario's Welfare Administration Act and Regulations and see the definition for "Assistance" above.)

Social Union:
An agreement, referred to as a SOCIAL UNION between the federal government and provincial governments, came into prominence during 1998 and the beginning of 1999. (See the "CONCLUSION" of A HISTORY OF THE CANADA ASSISTANCE PLAN).

Spokespersons:
Persons speaking or writing, usually on behalf of a cause or on behalf of a person or group of persons.

Stabilization:
In economics, the word refers mainly to an economic condition which never ideally exists, because many determinants affect the economy.

Supply and Demand:
These words used in theories of ECONOMICS refer to goods and services.

Transfixed:
Exceptional events and phenomena transfix attention.

Trends:
This history of The Canada Assistance Plan isn't an audit, although explanations are made about some of the changes of formats of expenditure records of Canada's Public Accounts, and Ontario's Public Accounts, (Ontario expenditures are used here as example of trends in each Province of Canada), which were most times changing from year to year. This study's purposes of recording data from 1966 to 1996 are to illustrate trends as expenditures were growing year by year. Although formats from year to year aren't consistent, records presenting upward expenditures' trends are pertinent and significant. Municipal, operating budgets of Metro Toronto, for example, were especially inconsistent over the same interval 1966 to 1996, in presentations without historical continuity. Yet, available budgetary records from those years are pertinent and significant. (See definition of "Mill rates".)

Truth:
Correct information is required for truth. Final truth isn't yet known. These definitions can't go into untruths - see the definitions of "Rhetoric".

Understanding:
My uses of the word in this study defines "understanding" in contexts where it is used.

Welfare:
Welfare was the original word referring to governmental benefits and allowances to persons in need, as distinguished from "Relief" which was by way of food or vouchers for food. The word "welfare" continues to be used, for example, in the General Welfare Assistance Act of Ontario which is an act of social services. And, in Metropolitan Toronto, for example, the original Department known as the Welfare Department became the Department of Social Services, and subsequently became the Department of Community and Social Services. (See "Assistance")

Welfare Services
In policies and administration referring to costs, "welfare services" refers to expenditures for administration and for programs such as Counselling and Work Activity which aren't expenditures for "assistance".[5]

Will:
Usage here isn't particularly concerned with criteria of "Last Will and Testament". Use of the word, "will" defines the word in this history of THE CANADA ASSISTANCE PLAN, CHAPTER 4: METAPHORS OF PUBLIC ADMINISTRATION. According to H. G. Wells' THE OUTLINE OF HISTORY, history has had many ups and downs with what has been known as a "community of will".[6]

FOOTNOTES OF THE GLOSSARY

1. THE GREAT CODE, THE BIBLE AND LITERATURE, by Northrop Frye, published by the Penguin Group, Penguin Books of Canada Limited, 10 Alcorn Avenue, Toronto, Ontario, Canada, M4V 3B2; ISBN 0-14-012928-6 260 pages. pp.135-38

2. SOCIAL SECURITY STATISTICS, CANADA AND PROVINCES, 1968-69 to 1992-93, published by authority of the Minister of Human Resources Development Canada, and is available from the Minister of Supply and Services Canada 1994. Cat. No. MT90-2/ 17-1993, ISBN 0-662-61662-6 And SOCIAL SECURITY STATISTICS, CANADA AND PROVINCES, 1970-71 to 1994-95, published by authority of Minister of Human Resources Development, Cat. No. MP90-2/ 17-1995, ISBN 0-662-62742-3

3. Canada Assistance Plan, Annual report, 1993-1994, Copyright under Minister of Public Works and Government Services Canada 1995, Cat. No. H75-8/1994; ISBN 0662-61711-8, SDHW-002-11-95

4. 1997 OPERATING PLAN AND BUDGET OF METROPOLITAN TORONTO

5. Canada Assistance Plan, Annual report, 1993-1994

6. THE OUTLINE OF HISTORY, by H. G. Wells, Revised and brought up to date by Raymond Postgate, Volumes I and II, Garden City Books, Garden City New York, copyright by Doubleday and Company 1961. ("Will, community of", is indexed six times.)

MINISTERS OF FINANCE, CANADA[1]
1966 to 1996

Hon. M.W. Sharp
November 1965 to April 1968

Hon. E.G. Benson
April 1968 to January 1972

Hon. J.N. Turner
January 1972 to September 1975

Hon. D.S. MacDonald
September 1975 to September 1977

Hon. J. J. Chrétien
September 1977 to June 1979

Hon. J.C. Crosbie
June 1979 to March 1980

Hon. A.J. MacEachen
April 1980 to September 1982·

Hon. M. Lalonde
September 1982 to September 1984

Hon. M.H. Wilson
September 1984 to April 1991

Hon. D.F. Mazankowski
April 1991 to June 1993

Hon. P. Martin
November 1993 to Present

A photo of a former Minister of Finance is unavailable.
Hon. G. Loiselle - Minister from June 1993 to November 1993

Source of Photos - Library of Parliament, Ottawa
Permission to use photos from Minister of Public Works and Government Services Canada
1999

CONTENTS OF THE APPENDICES

APPENDICES I & II
REVIEWS/REPORTS OF ACADEMIC STUDIES

APPENDICES III, IV & V
STATISTICS CANADA

APPENDICES VI, VII, VIII, IX & X
FINANCIAL AND OTHER DATA INFORMATION

APPENDIX 1 & 11: REVIEWS/REPORTS OF ACADEMIC STUDIES

APPENDIX I

PUBLIC ADMINISTRATION IN CANADA, SELECTED READINGS, by W.D.K. KERNAGHAN & A.M. WILLMS, printed and bound in Canada, Methuen Publications, second edition, 1970, 481 pages.ISBN 0-458-90790-1[1]. All following quotations here in the appendix are from the selected readings, by page numbers.

CHAPTER ONE, "Public Administration and Organization Theory" introduces the first article as follows, "The scope of the study of public administration has broadened so greatly during the post-war period that a brief definition of the subject is now impracticable."..."Dwight Waldo begins this book by examining the enduring problem of definition."

Article #1, "What is Public Administration?" by Dwight Waldo considers two typical definitions:

"(1) Public Administration is the organization and management of men and materials to achieve the purpose of government.

(2) Public Administration is the art and science of management as applied to affairs of state.

These are the ways public administration is usually defined. There is nothing wrong with such definitions - except that in themselves they do not help much in advancing understanding." p. 4. Approaching problems of definition and conditions of Public Administration, Dwight Waldo concluded, "Students of administration now know that they are not going to take heaven by storm, that is to say, quickly reduce human affairs to rule and chart. Some of them, even without ceasing to desire for more rationality than we have now achieved, are heard to say that complete rationality in human affairs is not the proper goal; that in a world in which all is orderly and predictable, with no room for spontaneity, surprise and emotional play, is an undesireable world." p. 16. I have to leave that concluding comment, as is, without elaboration, given the time span, and the many changes now confronting Public Administration since D. Waldo concluded his study. But I should refer to some of his other comments which bear upon some of my commentaries about Public Administration. "We might take the common-sense approach and ask simply, Does the government carry on the function or activity? For many common-sense purposes this is quite adequate...But for many purposes of study, analysis and informed action it is quite inadequate."..."The most fruitful approach to the meaning and significance of public for the student of administration is through the use of certain concepts which have been developed most fully in such disciplines as sociology and anthropology. The ones suggested as being particularly useful are associated with the expression structural-functional analysis and culture." p. 11. (i.e. p.11 in the Kernaghan and Willms text)

Would input/output of public consultation be out of context?

In the 1960s, volunteer organizations, and volunteers were often recruited to assist established organizations, but there wasn't nearly the emphasis on public consultation as there is in the 1990s. In the 1960s and earlier decades studies of the text edited by Kernaghan and Willms, weren't concerned with public inputs into Public Administration, although some of its writers acknowledged concerns for person-centred management. The text by Kernaghan and Siegel concentrated on conditions and issues of organizations and management in public administration. But at the same time, Dwight Waldo's article commenting upon the development of atomic energy as public, Waldo would ask, "Shall we call development programs carried on under contract by Union Carbide and Carbon Corporation public administration?"p. 11.

Included in the text PUBLIC ADMINISTRATION IN CANADA, SELECTED READINGS, theory as an issue was described in "THE MANAGEMENT THEORY JUNGLE REVISITED" by Donald Woolf, "pre-Christian writings about management subjects...such as Kautilya's ARTHASASTRA...ESSENTIALS OF INDIAN STATECRAFT ...Plato's REPUBLIC...and in the OLD TESTAMENT...more recently Gibbon's DECLINE AND FALL OF THE ROMAN EMPIRE...all treat with familiar management topics such as the chain of command, the span of control, and the specialization of labor." p. 20. "A good theory provides us with reasonably reliable means of prediction."..."A theory of management (and, by implication, organizations) should define why we have it, what it is, and how it works." p. 17. Woolf leads into two approaches to management theory,

1. Organization-centred theory
2. Person-centred theory. p. 19.

Organization-centred theory hasn't been unanimously approved in organizations, and person-centered theories introduced in the 1930s offered departures from organization-centred theories. "Interestingly enough, a truly "eclectic " theory has not emerged from the efforts of theorists working from comparatively divergent viewpoints...

"Firstly, the assumptions of the theories regarding human behaviour and the nature of man are virtually irreconcilable. Organization-centred theory treats people as subsidiary to the organization and comparable to other necessary resources and commodities, i.e., their behaviour and needs will be modified to meet the needs of the organization. Moreover, the motives of people are probably suspect. By contrast, person-centred theorists start with people as the focal point, and propose modifying organizational structure and goals to meet human needs.

The second basic reason for the failure of an eclectic theory is that theorists writing from divergent viewpoints do not appear to use the same vocabulary or address themselves to the same questions. Indeed, their occasional apparent hostility to opposing viewpoints would seem to preclude their doing this. Therefore, until some agreement on these two vital issues is reached, management theory will continue to be a "jungle." p. 27.

PUBLIC ADMINISTRATION IN CANADA, SELECTED READINGS, next offer "The Proverbs of Administration" by Herbert Simon a study that was written in 1946 in the journal, PUBLIC ADMINISTRATION REVIEW, Vol. 6, 1946. Simon's study critically examined administrative principles which were believed to be effective for administrative efficiency - namely,

1. specialization among the group
2. a determinate hierarchy of authority
3. limiting span of control at any point in the hierarchy
4. grouping the workers for purposes of control, according to (a) purpose, (b) process, (c) clientele, or (d) place. Simon noted (This is really an elaboration of the first principle.) p. 28.

Further, according to Simon, "Purpose, process, clientele and place are competing bases of organization, and at any given point of division the advantages of three must be sacrificed to secure the advantages of the fourth." Adjustments in organization can correct imbalances among the competing bases, but the adjustments entangle specialization criteria at the next level in the organization. "Here again is posed the dilemma of choosing between alternate, equally plausible, administrative principles. But this is not the only difficulty in the present case, for closer study of the situation shows there are fundamental ambiguities in the meanings of the key terms - "purpose, process, clientele and place." pp. 31-32. Simon goes on to explain the ambiguites. In conclusion, he stated, "Unity of command, specialization by purpose, decentralization are all items to be considered in the design of an efficient administrative organization. No single one of these items is of sufficient importance to suffice as a guiding principle for the administrative analyst. In the design of administrative organizations, as in their operation, over-all efficiency must be the guiding criteria." p. 35. ("Purpose" in organization theory, as above, isn't like "Purpose" in the Y.M.C.A.; see Chapter 4.)

Following the article by Herbert Simon, the text reprinted an article from PUBLIC ADMINISTRATION (U.K.) Vol. 44, Winter 1966, "The Classical Organization Theory and Its Critics", by V. Subramaniam who revealed two strands of criticism of the classical theory, "(i) those which attack the inconsistancies, tautologies and lack of sophistication of the formulations of classical theorists -initiated mainly by Simon, and (ii) those which take issue with the pro-management bias of classical theory." p. 37. In conclusion, Subramaniam refers to "The Teacher's Problem" with intellectual shortcomings of classical organization theory which "owes much of its success to its combination of 'practical' and 'theoretical' knowledge in an unacademic way". "The knowledge itself is stated in vague but suggestive language. The statements often do not amount to more than some refined proverbial wisdom and some useful tips on technique but their effect on the receptive student may be out of all proportion to the intellectual quality of the statements themselves." "The success of the classical theory with managers depends more on this suggestive potentiality and less on its intellectual content."pp.45-46.

Here follows a review/report about "Planning and Finance" in Chapter Eight. Article #24 is by A.M. WILLMS, "The Theory of Planning" pp.250-259.

To quote from this article which was written about 30 years ago, "Very little research has been done on planning." ...."When practical data become available in quantity managers will be able to confirm by analysis the ideas we now broach as concepts or suggestions. It is a measure of the preponderance of art over science in management that we must be content with ideas which, though popular, may on practical testing turn out to be half truths or even myths."

WILLMS went on from there through the following sections:

"PLANNING AS A MANAGEMENT FUNCTION."
"1. AIMS AND POLICY"
"2. ASSESSING ALTERNATIVES"
"3. ARRANGING FOR NECESSARY RESOURCES"
"4. OUTLINE OF THE ORGANIZATION, METHODS AND PROCEDURES"
"5. THE PLAN"

"WHY PLAN?"
"SOME LIMITATIONS TO PLANNING"

Amidst the substance of many concise comments, WILLMS quoted J.D. MILLETT, "The planner must know what is as part of what should be." p. 254. The quote is pertinent to highlight phenomena of planning. In reading the substance of the article, we're involved with abstract planning materials which are separate from actual planning, except where examples are made. Who in the world would use the substance presented here for a check list to be followed in the real world of planning? Yet the substance is compelling, and another example might help us along the way beyond the text. For example, the real world where forests still exist, presents to forestery planners "what is as part of what should be" very differently than the real world of municipal planners of say, the village of Flesherton, Ontario before and after their first sewage system was installed in 1994.

Another quote from WILLMS carries us onward beyond the time 30 years ago when he wrote the article, "In long-term planning a point may be reached where the forecasting is not accurate enough to justify peering farther into the future. There is an inverse relation between distance of projection and accuracy - the greater the time span the more chance for the unexpected - and reliability diminishes quickly. Sophisticated forecasting will help determine the amount of feasible planning." p. 259

However, three of today's dominant preoccupations couldn't be forecasted 30 years ago, namely
1.   Tremendous growth of information technology used by administrative management in public services in the 1990s.
2.   30 years ago, it couldn't be forecasted there would be such massive deficits and debts of governments in the 1990s.

3. It's unlikely readers etched in memory the following question begging comment of mine. I think it significant to repeat here this preoccupation which is subliminally felt,

"It's a good thing we have enduring Acts, Regulations and Policies, as organizations terminate."

FOOTNOTES TO APPENDIX I:

1. PUBLIC ADMINISTRATION IN CANADA, SELECTED READINGS, by W.D.K. KERNAGHAN & A.M. WILLMS, printed and bound in Canada, Methuen Publications, second edition, 1971, 481 pages. ISBN 0-458-90790-1

APPENDIX II

1987 SECOND EDITION by Kernaghan and Siegel.

PUBLIC ADMINISTRATION IN CANADA, A TEXT, Second Edition, edited by Kenneth Kernaghan and David Siegel, published by Methuen, Toronto 1987, 642 pages.[1]

This text is a more extensive publication than the book by Kernaghan and Willms which I reviewed here in APPENDIX I. By the way, references in the 1971 text by Kernaghan and Willms about schools of human relations, or person-centredness, (eg. Theory Y) are indexed under "Organizational Humanism" in the Kernaghan and Siegel text. Other differences of their text, as compared with similar studies, haven't been researched here. Kernaghan & Siegel's text is so extensive a study of Public Administration, instead of researching and reviewing it, I've quoted pp. ix to xviii from their complete "DETAILED TABLE OF CONTENTS", with the consents of the authors Kenneth Kernaghan and David Siegel.

The following "DETAILED TABLE OF CONTENTS", quoted from pages ix to xviii of the text by Kernaghan and Siegel, is sequenced with the text, according to titles of subjects and sub-subjects in the ways the titles appear on each page.

DETAILED TABLE OF CONTENTS

Public Administration versus Private Administration
The Study of Public Administration
Political Science or Administrative Science?
Public Administration as Public Administration
The Environment and Expansion of Canadian Bureacracy
Environmental Factors
The Growth of Public Bureaucracy
The Evolution and Interpretation of Public Bureaucracy
Origins and Criticisms of Public Bureaucracy
Bureaucratic Theories
Bibliography

2. Public Administration and Organization Theory:
The Structural Foundation
Max Weber and Classical Bureaucratic Theory
The Characteristics of Weberian Bureaucracy
Criticisms of Weber
Conclusion
Bibliography
Cases

3. Public Administration and Organizational Theory:
The Humanistic Response
Organizational Humanism
Mary Parker Follett
Roethlesbereger and Dickson and the Hawthorne Experiments
Chester Barnard and the Importance of Cooperation
Abraham Maslow's Hierarchy of Needs
Douglas MacGregor's Theory X and Theory Y
Summary of Principles of Organizational Humanism
Criticism of Organizational Humanism
Participatory Management
Management by Objectives
Organizational Development
The Canadian Experience: From Taylor to MBO
Katz and Kahn's Open System Approach
Contingency Theory
The Future of Organizations
Conclusions
Bibliography
Cases

4. Motivation, Leadership and Communication
   Communications
      Different Kinds of Communication
      Obstacles to Communications
   Leadership
      Leadership Traits or Skills
      Styles of Leadership: Authoritarian, Democratic, Laisse-faire
      Contingency Theories
   Motivation
      Chris Argyris's Maturity-Immaturity Theory
      Frederick Herzberg's Motivation-Hygiene Theory
      Job Redesign
      Quality of Working Life
      Theory Z - Japanese Management
      Can Theory Z Work in Canada?
      In Search of Excellence
         Conclusion and an Assessment
   Bibliography
   Cases

5. Making and Implementing Public Policy
   Models of Policy Making
      Comprehensive Rationality
      Incrementalism
      Bounded Rationality and Satisficing
      Mixed Scanning
      Public Choice
      Governmental or Bureaucratic Politics
      Socio-economic Determinants
      Marxist Analysis
   Implementation
      The Implemetation Process
      Difficulties of Implementation
      The Choice of Governing Instrument
   Bibliography
   Cases

Part II: The Choice of Organizational Form

6. Government Departments and Central Agencies
   The Choice of Organizational Form
   The Legislature, the Executive, and Departments
      Definition of a Department

The Public Interest
The Meaning of the Public Interest
Determining the Public Interest
Administrative Responsibility and the Public Interest
Bibliography
Cases

13. The Executive and the Bureaucracy
Coordination and Ministerial Responsibility
Ministerial Responsibility
Coordination and Hierarchy
The Key Role of the Deputy Minister
The Prime Minister and the Cabinet
The Prime Minister
Cabinet Committees
Central Agencies
The Policy and Expenditure Management System
Cabinet Approval and Cabinet Documents
Bibliography
Cases

14. Interdepartmental and Intradepartmental Relations
Departmental and Agency Interaction
Interdepartmental Committees
Departments and Central Agencies
Interdepartmental Relations
The Deputy Minister
Ministerial Staff
Departmental Management
Concluding Observations
Bibliography
Cases

15. The Legislature and the Bureaucracy
Ministerial Responsibility and Political Neutrality
The Resignation of Ministers
The Answerability of Ministers
Legislative Control and Influence
Watchdog Agencies
Legislative Committees
Bibliography
Cases

FOOTNOTES TO APPENDIX II: regarding Second Edition by Kernaghan and Siegel, see footnote below.

1995 THIRD EDITION by Kernaghan and Siegel:

PUBLIC ADMINISTRATION IN CANADA, A TEXT, Third Edition, edited by Kenneth Kernaghan and David Siegel, published by Nelson, Toronto 1995, 706 pages.[2]

The Third Edition is much the same as the Second Edition of PUBLIC ADMINISTRATION IN CANADA by Kenneth Kernaghan and David Seigel but with amendments and additions (See PART I of APPENDIX II reviewed above). Each chapter of the Third Edition has some amendments, and the final chapter is new - "PART VII: The Future of Public Administration". Quoting from the 1995 Third Edition, is especially significant to a study of Public Admininistration, "The making of decisions and recommendations on complex and technical matters of "social planning" requires the exercise of discretionary powers of a legislative and judicial nature. Further, the participation of officials in negotiation, bargaining, compromise and reconciliation in order to "break a political deadlock" is undeniably political activity."[3]

The composition of the Third Edition text includes a Preface and Introduction; the final pages, formatted the same way as the Second Edition, are abbreviated here as following,

Appendix: How to Write a Research Paper in Public Administration

Glossary
Name Index
Subject Index

<u>FOOTNOTES TO APPENDIX II,</u>

1. <u>PUBLIC ADMINISTRATION IN CANADA,</u> A TEXT, Second Edition, by Kenneth Kernaghan and David Siegel, published by Methuen Publications, Toronto 1987, 642 pages, 1987
ISBN 0-458-80650-1, pp. 105-106

2. <u>PUBLIC ADMINISTRATION IN CANADA,</u> A TEXT, Third Edition by Kenneth Kernaghan and David Siegel, published by Nelson Canada, Toronto, 1995, ISBN 0-17-604187-7

3. Ibid p.332

Population Growth, by Province, for Census Periods 1901-56, All ages.

Province	1901	1911	Change 1901–11	1921	Change 1911–21	1931	Change 1921–31
	No.	No.	p.c.	No.	p.c.	No.	p.c.
Newfoundland......	—	—	—	—	—	—	—
Prince Edward Is...	103,259	93,728	−9.2	88,615	−5.5	88,038	−0.7
Nova Scotia........	459,574	492,338	7.1	523,837	6.4	512,846	−2.1
New Brunswick.....	331,120	351,889	6.3	387,876	10.2	408,219	5.2
Quebec...........	1,648,898	2,005,776	21.6	2,360,510	17.7	2,874,662	21.8
Ontario...........	2,182,947	2,527,292	15.8	2,933,662	16.1	3,431,683	17.0
Manitoba........	255,211	461,394	80.8	610,118	32.2	700,139	14.8
Saskatchewan.....	91,279	492,432	439.5	757,510	53.8	921,785	21.7
Alberta...........	73,022	374,295	412.6	588,454	57.2	731,605	24.3
British Columbia...	178,657	392,480	119.7	524,582	33.7	694,263	32.3
Canada¹.......	**5,371,315**	**7,206,643**	**34.2**	**8,787,949**	**21.9**	**10,376,786**	**18.1**

Province	1941	Change 1931–41	1951	Change 1941–51	1956	Change 1951–56
	No.	p.c.	No.	p.c.	No.	p.c.
Newfoundland...............	—	—	361,416	—	415,074	14.8
Prince Edward Is...........	95,047	8.0	98,429	3.6	99,285	0.9
Nova Scotia...............	577,962	12.7	642,584	11.2	694,717	8.1
New Brunswick............	457,401	12.0	515,697	12.7	554,616	7.5
Quebec..................	3,331,882	15.9	4,055,681	21.7	4,628,378	14.1
Ontario..................	3,787,655	10.4	4,597,542	21.4	5,404,933	17.6
Manitoba.................	729,744	4.2	776,541	6.4	850,040	9.5
Saskatchewan.............	895,992	−2.8	831,728	−7.2	880,665	5.9
Alberta..................	796,169	8.8	939,501	18.0	1,123,116	19.5
British Columbia...........	817,861	17.8	1,165,210	42.5	1,398,464	20.0
Canada¹.................	**11,506,655**	**10.9**	**14,009,429**	**21.8**	**16,080,791**	**14.8**

¹ Includes the Yukon and Northwest Territories.

Some census information from Statistics Canada includes tables of data about non-institutionalized persons. Such data need to be supplemented for records about the Canada Assistance Plan, which was mostly with non-institutionalized persons, but also concerned with institutionalized persons. Population information about institutionalized persons dependent on the Canada Assistance Plan, as residents of Homes of Special Care, is available from the catalogues of SOCIAL SECURITY STATISTICS as published by Human Resources Development Canada as indicated in numbered Tables,

411 Number of Beds in Homes for Special Care for Adults
414 Number of Beds in Homes for Special Care for Children[1]

Also, see APPENDIX VI: CANADA ASSISTANCE PLAN ANNUAL REPORTS for data under the heading "NUMBERS OF PERSONS ASSISTED", including "Persons In Homes for Special Care - Adults and Children".[2] Most institutionalized persons, in hospitals, weren't shareable under the Canada Assistance Plan.

In this history of THE CANADA ASSISTANCE PLAN, no attempt is made here to correlate any statistical information, except as follows, populations data correlates to the labour force, employed and unemployed persons, and persons not in the labour force; the data for 1966 to 1997 - includes the years 1966 to 1996 of The Canada Assistance Plan's existence. Data transcibed for here from Statistics Canada sources in totals of males plus females is from "Males and Females" data. Age 15 years and over.

APPENDIX III: (a) POPULATION STATISTICS, LABOUR FORCE, AND EMPLOYED PERSONS. [3]

Data of employed persons Agricultural plus Non-agricultural, males plus females, all such are reported here in totals. Data by thousands (000). Sources are recorded via footnotes.

	POPULATION (000) Civilian Non-institutional	LABOUR FORCE (000)	EMPLOYED PERSONS (000)
1966	13,083	7,493	7,242
1967	13,444	7,747	7,451
1968	13,805	7,950	7,593
1969	14,162	8,194	7,832
1970	14,528	8,395	7,919
1971	14,872	8,639	8,104
1972	15,186	8,897	8,344
1973	15,526	9,276	8,759
1974	15,924	9,639	9,125
1975	16,323	9,974	9,284
1976	17,123.5	10,530.0	9,776.1
1977	17,493.0	10,860.3	9,978.2
1978	17,839.0	11,264.9	10,320.3
1979	18,182.7	11,630.3	10,760.6
1980	18,549.6	11,982.6	11,082.2
1981	18,883.3	12,331.9	11,398.0
1982	19,176.8	12,397.9	11,035.1
1983	19,433.3	12,609.9	11,105.7
1984	19,680.5	12,852.6	11,402.4
1985	19,929.5	13,122.8	11,741.9
1986	20,182.1	13,377.7	12,094.5
1987	20,432.4	13,630.6	12,422.4
1988	20,689.6	13,900.5	12,818.9
1989	20,967.6	14,151.3	13,086.0
1990	21,277.4	14,329.0	13,165.1
1991	21,612.7	14,407.8	12,916.1
1992	21,986.2	14,482.2	12,842.0
1993	22,371.3	14,663.5	13,014.7
1994	22,716.8	14,832.4	13,291.7
1995	23,027.3	14,927.6	13,505.5
1996	23,351.8	15,145.4	13,676.2
1997	23,686.5	15,354.0	13,940.6

Canada's Social Security is part of the context arising from the Constitution of Canada. Social Security, per se, in retrospect will likely be irrelevant in a few generations hence as population changes will create altogether different contexts than hitherto known in Canada. "Population projections should be made only after extensive study of the patterns and trends of the past. In many cases they are inadvisable. But freqently the demand for estimates of future population is such that they must be made."[4] This study of the Canada Assistance Plan cannot possibly make extensive studies of patterns and trends of Canada's past. However, data from Statistics Canada as presented here does provide a foundation for extensive studies of patterns and trends, pertinent to Social Security in Canada.

STATISTICS CANADA continued:
APPENDIX III: (b) EMPLOYED PERSONS, NOT GOVERNMENT EMPLOYEES & GOVERNMENT EMPLOYEES: data thousands[5]

	POPULATION NOT IN INSTITUTIONS (000)	NOT GOVERNMENT EMPLOYEES (000)	GOVERNMENT EMPLOYEES (000)
1966	13,474	data	data
1967	13,873	unavailable	unavailable
1968	14,264	"	"
1969	14,638	"	"
1970	15,016	"	"
1971	15,388	"	"
1972	15,747	"	"
1973	16,124	"	"
1974	16,562	"	"
1975	17,019	"	"
1976	17,123.5	8,569.5	1,913.9
1977	17,493.0	8,698.2	1,990.5
1978	17,839.0	8,960.1	2,005.1
1979	18,182.7	9,337.7	1,925.2
1980	18,549.6	9,619.9	1,966.1
1981	18,883.3	9,876.6	2,006.5
1982	19,176.8	9,498.0	2,031.9
1983	19,433.3	9,511.5	2,074.3
1984	19,680.5	9,773.6	2.080.5
1985	19,929.5	10,065.0	2,097.5
1986	20,182.1	10,412.9	2,127.9
1987	20,432.4	10,676.3	2,143.1
1988	20,689.6	10,998.0	2,193.3
1989	20,967.6	11,276.9	2,166.3
1990	21,277.4	11,275.8	2,148.0
1991	21,612.7	10,996.2	2,173.0
1992	21,986.2	10,905.8	2,219.0
1993	22,371.3	10,958.4	2,198.4
1994	22,716.8	11,180.3	2,195.7
1995	23,027.3	11,369.9	2,107.4
1996	23,351.8	11,409.6	2,098.4
1997	23,686.5	11,452.6	2,066.1

APPENDIX IV: (a) LABOUR FORCE, EMPLOYED AND UNEMPLOYED PERSONS: data by thousands (000).[6]

	LABOUR FORCE (000)	EMPLOYED PERSONS (000)	UNEMPLOYED PERSONS (000)
1966	7,493	7,242	251
1967	7,747	7,451	296
1968	7,951	7,593	358
1969	8,194	7,832	362
1970	8,395	7,919	476
1971	8,639	8,104	535
1972	8,897	8,344	553
1973	9,276	8,761	515
1974	9,639	9,125	514
1975	9,974	9,284	690
1976	10,530.0	9,776.1	753.9
1977	10,860.3	9,978.2	882.1
1978	11,264.9	10,320.3	944.5
1979	11,630.3	10,760.6	869.7
1980	11,982.6	11,082.2	900.4
1981	12,331.9	11,398.0	933.9
1982	12,397.9	11,035.1	1,362.8
1983	12,609.9	11,105.7	1,504.2
1984	12,852.6	11,402.4	1,450.2
1985	13,122.8	11,741.9	1,380.8
1986	13,377.7	12,094.5	1,283.1
1987	13,630.6	12,422.4	1,208.2
1988	13,900.5	12,818.9	1,081.6
1989	14,151.3	13,086.0	1,065.3
1990	14,329.0	13,165.1	1,163.9
1991	14,407.8	12,916.1	1,491.7
1992	14,482.2	12,842.0	1,640.2
1993	14,663.5	13,014.7	1,648.8
1994	14,832.4	13,291.7	1,540.7
1995	14,927.6	13,505.5	1,422.1
1996	15,145.4	13,676.2	1,469.2
1997	15,354.0	13,940.6	1,413.5

APPENDIX IV: (b) "LABOUR FORCE" and "NOT IN THE LABOUR FORCE":
data by thousands (000).[7]

	POPULATION (000) Civilian Non-institutional	LABOUR FORCE (000)	PERSONS NOT IN LABOUR FORCE (000)
1966	13,083	7,493	5,590
1967	13,444	7,747	5,697
1968	13,805	7,951	5,854
1969	14,162	8,194	5,968
1970	14,528	8,395	6,133
1971	14,872	8,639	6,233
1972	15,186	8,897	6,289
1973	15,526	9,276	6,250
1974	15,924	9,639	6,285
1975	16,323	9,974	6,349
1976	17,123.5	10,530.0	6,593.5
1977	17,493.0	10,860.3	6,632.7
1978	17,839.0	11,264.9	6,574.1
1979	18,182.7	11,630.3	6,552.4
1980	18,549.6	11,982.6	6,567.1
1981	18,883.3	12,331.9	6,551.4
1982	19,176.8	12,397.9	6,778.9
1983	19,433.3	12,609.9	6,823.4
1984	19,680.5	12,852.6	6,827.9
1985	19,929.5	13,122.8	6,806.7
1986	20,182.1	13,377.7	6,804.4
1987	20,432.4	13,630.6	6,801.7
1988	20,689.6	13,900.5	6,789.1
1989	20,967.6	14,151.3	6,816.3
1990	21,277.4	14,329.0	6,948.3
1991	21,612.7	14,407.8	7,204.9
1992	21,986.2	14,482.2	7,504.0
1993	22,371.3	14,663.5	7,707.8
1994	22,716.8	14,832.4	7,884.4
1995	23,027.3	14,927.6	8,099.7
1996	23,351.8	15,145.4	8,206.5
1997	23,686.5	15,534.0	8,332.5

APPENDIX V: 1991 CENSUS BY PROVINCES - ALL AGES

Newfoundland	568,000
Prince Edward Island	130,000
Nova Scotia	900,000
New Brunswick	724,000
Quebec	6,895,000
Ontario	10,085,000
Manitoba	1,092,000
Saskatchewan	988,000
Alberta	2,546,000
British Columbia	3,282,000
Total	27,210,000

Source: Statistics Canada

FOOTNOTES FOR APPENDIX III, IV & V: STATISTICS CANADA

1. SOCIAL SECURITY STATISTICS, CANADA AND PROVINCES, 1968-69 TO 1992-93, and 1970-71 to 1994-95, published by authority of the Minister of Human Resources Development Canada, and is available from the Minister of Supply and Services Canada 1994.
   Cat. No. MT90-2/17-1993, ISBN 0-662-61662-6
   Cat. No. MP90-2/17-1995, ISBN 0-662-62742-3

2. CANADA ASSISTANCE PLAN ANNUAL REPORT(S), Published by authority Minister of Human Resources Development. Copies of the reports are available from the Enquiries Centre, Human Resources Development Canada, 140 Promenade du Portage, Portage IV, Level 0, Hull, Quebec K1A 0J9

3. 1996 CENSUS - STATISTICS CANADA CD ROM
   93F0029XDB96005 tab 01an.ivt:LF est. annual avg age group 15 + both sexes. & V0OT3OBU.ivt by class of worker, annual avg, both sexes, 1976 to 1997.

   LABOUR FORCE DATA 1966 to 1975, population 15 years and over, was supplied as estimates by Statistics Canada.

4. TECHNIQUES OF POPULATION ANALYSIS, by George W. Barclay, published by John Wiley and Sons, Inc. 1958, fifth printing 1965, Library of Congress Card #58-59899

5. 1996 CENSUS - STATISTICS CANADA CD ROM V0OT3OBU.ivt Emp. by class of worker, Both Sexes EMPLOYED PERSONS, NOT GOVERNMENT EMPLOYEES and GOVERNMENT EMPLOYEES

6. 1996 CENSUS - STATISTICS CANADA CD ROM
   93F0029XDB96005 tab 01an.ivt:LF est.

7. LABOUR FORCE DATA 1966 to 1975, population 15 years and over, was supplied as estimates by Statistics Canada.

APPENDICES VI, VII, VIII, IX, X FINANCIAL

<u>APPENDIX VI: CANADA ASSISTANCE PLAN ANNUAL REPORTS
& OTHER REPORTS REGARDING CAP.</u>

"Before the introduction of CAP in 1966, provinces received sharing of costs of social assistance through the following federal categorical programs which were targeted to specific groups or categories of people: Old Age Assistance, Blind Persons Allowance, Disabled Persons Allowance and Unemployment Assistance."[1]

The Annual Reports of the Canada Assistance Plan described the Components of CAP, and the descriptions included the following information.

General Assistance

The CAP Agreement stipulated certain requirements for cost sharing of assistance, that assistance was to be provided to "persons in need"; eligibility wasn't dependent on prior residence in a province; provincial laws had to provide for appeals regarding "assistance" decisions; the assistance provided was to be authorized as listed in Schedule C of the CAP Agreement. Basic requirements of "general assistance" included food, shelter, clothing, fuel, utilities, household supplies and personal requirements. Also provided were travel costs, transportation, funerals and burials, and comfort allowances for persons residing in hospitals or homes for special care. Various prescribed needs were also provided through CAP, such as incidental to carrying on a trade or other employment; and special needs of any kind, especially for safety, well-being or rehabilitation, including repairs or alterations to property; civil legal aid; and purchased day care services.

Homes for Special Care

Homes listed in Schedule A of the CAP Agreement, included 6 categories - Homes for the Aged, Nursing Homes, Hostels for Transients, Child Care Institutions, Homes for Unmarried Mothers, and Homes of Other Kinds. After 1977, long term residential care for adults was funded under Extended Health Care Services provisions of Federal-Provincial Fiscal Arrangements and Federal Post Secondary Education and Health Contributions Act.

Health Care

Certain health care costs for "persons in need" were cost shared by CAP if they weren't part of other provincial programs, or under other federal-provincial agreements.

Child Care

Children's Aid programs of foster homes was shared as assistance. Costs of facilities for children were covered under the homes for special care component. The remainder of costs were shared under Welfare Services.

Welfare Services

CAP shared services delivered by provincially approved agencies listed in Schedule B to the CAP Agreement for "persons in need" or for "persons likely to become in need". Services included adoptions, casework, counselling, assessments and referrals; community development; consulting, research and evaluation - re welfare programs; day-care services for children; homemakers, home support, etc; rehabilitation services; administrative services.

Work Activity Projects

Projects designed to assist persons who, because of personal, family or environmental barriers experience unusual difficulty.

More information about all the above components of the Canada Assistance Plan is provided in the Annual Reports.[2] Federal payments, and numbers of persons assisted under the CAP agreement, among other data reports, are outlined in the Annual Reports for 1982-83 onward, as follows.

FINANCIAL INFORMATION[3] ($000) (Federal Payments)

1982-83

Provnc	Genrl Assist	Hms SpcCr	Hlth Care	Child Welf.	Welf Serv.	Wrk Actv Prjs	Totals
Nfld	39,550	8,893	4,367	3,833	9,100	215	65,958
PEI	11,310	2,159	529	586	3,749		18,333
NS	58,969	10,602	1,102	2,126	13,273	397	86,469
NB	85,099	8,036	2,914	1,256	10,167	215	107,687
QU	742.871	198,210	39,642	27,983	157,236		1,165,942
ON	523,533	46,295	3,680	78,412	89,153	1,179	742,252
MAN	47,648	7,569	2,666	12,235	19,700	1,936	91,754
SAS	66,109	22,539	1,243	4,165	25,688	148	119,882
AL	183,710	35,287		35,593	50,851	220	305,661
BC	318,069	42,922	14,011	7,009	90,912	788	473,711
NWT	4,217	1,805	269	844	2,980		10,115
YU	1,451	7		215	977		2,650
Totals	2,082,536	384,324	70,423	174,257	473,786	5,098	3,190,424

1983-84 ($000)

Provnc	Genrl Assist	Hms SpcCr	Hlth Care	Child Welf.	Welf Serv. Prjs	Wrk Actv	Totals
Nfld	44,584	8,882	5,950	3,641	8,027	194	71,278
PEI	9,805	2,018	395	345	3,990		16,553
NS	62,272	10,497	990	1,745	17,192	354	93,050
NB	87,307	8,465	3,185	1,215	11,506		111,678
QUE	931,715	214,043	57,358	26,581	169,275	82	1,399,054*
ON	601,893	48,146	5,221	83,423	89,988	2,199	830,870
MAN	59,803	9,581	3,192	11,342	23,149	1,804	108,871
SAS	82,217	21,540	1,306	3,550	33,769	157	142,539
AL	200,660	35,755		34,494	54,864	247	326,020
BC	384,856	29,122	19,583	7,104	90,043	486	531,194
NWT	4,844	1,641	111	628	2,929		10,153
YU	904	29		137	571		1,641
Totals	2,470,860	389,719	97,291	174,205	505,303	5,523	3,642,901

* Federal contributions to Quebec includes tax transfers.

1984-85

Nfld	43,030	8,773	5,561	4,700	11,839	132	74,035
PEI	10,665	2,075	330	340	4,165		17,575
NS	69,730	12,839	2,954	1,952	16,693	505	104,673
NB	96,429	8,408	3,026	1,467	16,848	(2)	126,176
QU	1,027,717	205,210	62,511	25,942	191,735	37	1,513,152
ON	703,211	45,752	8,408	45,140	141,012		943,523
MAN	74,932	9,415	4,137	13,212	28,533	1,950	132,179
SAS	86,478	24,018	1,964	3,642	27,218	193	143,513
AL	209,805	34,382	31,406	58,449		244	334,286
BC	433,263	44,026	21,068	6,411	93,978	42	598,788
NWT	4,664	1,840		933	2,790		10,227
YU	1,020	33		322	1,049		2,424
Totals	2,760,944	396,711	109,959	135,467	594,309	3,101	4,000,551

1985-86

Nfld	42,577	8,514	5,598	4,573	14,318	128	75,708
PEI	11,205	2,779	436	506	5,808		20,734
NS	71,641	11,338	3,902	2,434	14,736	425	104,476
NB	103,362	7,800	4,598	1,800	19,348	(2)	136,906
QU	1,110,953	179,474	72,066	26,324	216,925	37	1,605,779
ON	739,739	73,258	23,298	49,839	165,880	344	1,052,358
MAN	78,414	9,620	4,129	13,359	34,039	1,745	141,306
SAS	95,367	12,092	2,547	4,184	34,264	176	148,630
AL	240,859	46,177	17,097	15,185	69,959	496	389,773
BC	439,523	41,298	19,792	3,510	88,390	960	593,473
NWT	5,482	1,974		923	3,197		11,576
YU	1,082	(82)	79	382	1,399		2,860
Totals	2,940,204	394,242	153,542	123,019	668,263	4,309	4,283,579

1986-87 ($000)

Provnc	Genrl Assist	Hms SpcCr	Hlth Care	Child Welf.	Welf Serv. Prjs	Wrk Actv	Totals
Nfld	53,982	6,134	7,110	5,288	12,868	98	85,480
PEI	11,621	2,751	862	466	4,080		19,780
NS	81,728	14,355	4,557	3,633	19,920	213	124,406
NB	114,641	4,983	4,630	3,084	17,770		145,108
QU	1,073,371	132,104	82,103	21,817	236,402		1,545,797
ON	821,407	52,938	10,480	36,456	209,467	1,101	1,132,209
MAN	89,917	10,445	4,622	9,382	38,157	2,058	154,581
SAS	107,734	12,107	2,765	4,392	33,548	159	160,705
AL	271,719	38,359	24,763	12,615	78,572	237	426,265
BC	429,872	41,312	29,105	6,375	125,323	69	623,056
NWT	5,998	1,350		1,105	3,551		12,004
YU							
Totals	3,061,990	316,838	171,357	104,613	779,658	3,935	4,438,391

1987-88

	Genrl Assist	Hms SpcCr	Hlth Care	Child Welf.	Welf Serv. Prjs	Wrk Actv	Totals
Nfld	53,900	5,742	8,897	6,141	13,725	(6)	88,399
PEI	12,280	3,122	976	601	4,706		21,729
NS	89,231	12,822	5,440	5,201	15,606	350	128,650
NB	117,519	4,167	6,528	2,990	21,146		152,350
QU	1,059,048	200,984	73,942	24,043	222,846		1,580,863
ON	915,730	41,376	31,605	51,777	278,510	849	1,319,847
MAN	88,912	13,691	4,954	9,954	44,921	1,762	164,194
SAS	107,475	13,204	2,211	4,424	30,049	185	157,548
AL	296,523	25,417	26,630	15,610	78,231	471	442,882
BC	447,571	41,927	33,285	2,144	127,515	345	652,787
NWT	8,105	1,369		1,282	3,220		13,976
YU	669	616		393	1,437		3,115
Totals	3,196,963	364,481	194,468	124,560	841,912	3,956	4,726,340

1988-89

	Genrl Assist	Hms SpcCr	Hlth Care	Child Welf.	Welf Serv. Prjs	Wrk Actv	Totals
Nfld	54,640	6,366	8,233	6,572	15,532	10	91,353
PEI	12,455	2,589	997	795	5,766		22,602
NS	102,453	12,588	6,086	4,880	25,754	1,108	152,869
NB	113,768	5,717	6,148	3,212	20,944		149,789
QU	1,060,727	225,875	78,118	26,368	262,695		1,653,783
ON	1,062,212	54,252	43,783	72,091	277,441	1,191	1,510,970
MAN	109,561	14,710	6,812	13,203	51,409	2,082	197,777
SAS	100,067	12,484	1,521	4,892	36,037	(152)	155,153
AL	327,863	34,322	27,207	18,432	79,684	362	487,870
BC	439,187	55,377	33,257	4,329	130.962		663,112
NWT	7,189	1,955		1,523	4,336		15,003
YU	3,036	966		597	3,512		8,111
Total	3,393,158	427,201	212,162	156,894	914,072	4,905	5,108,392

1989-90 ($000)

Provnc	Genrl Assist	Hms SpcCr	Hlth Care	Child Welf.	Welf Serv. Prjs	Wrk Actv	Totals
Nfld	59,609	6,277	8,686	8,072	18,405		101,049
PEI	13,748	2,817	918	775	5,623		23,881
NS	109,951	15,332	6,888	5,928	18,280	832	157,211
NB	118,092	6,234	6,020	3,556	25,034	158,936	
QU	1,071,979	209,675	83,357	5,456	332,487	656	1,173,610
ON	1,212,573	49,657	64,795	6,806	387,493	158	1,761,482
MAN	103,163	16,466	6,694	13,267	52,629	2,278	194,497
SAS	94,643	14,679	4,742	6,911	31,793	89	152,857
AL	341,729	41,285	30,015	19,031	80,888	239	513,187
BC	436,157	58,480	31,874	3,666	163,259	347	693,783
NWT	10,129	1,905		1,479	3,346		16,859
YU	1,386	620		461	2,735		5,202
Totals	3,573,159	423,427	243,989	135,408	1,121,972	4,599	5,502,554

1990-91

Nfl	71,255	7,388	11,481	8,622	20,221	-	118,967
PEI	16,546	3,010	1,174	809	7,190	-	28,729
NS	124,632	15,234	7,711	8,097	33,144	271	189,089
NB	130,526	5,964	6,831	3,895	26,527	-	73,743
Qu	1,204,289	212,745	91,177	28,493	363,062	-	1,899,766
On	1,819,595	77,267	95,861	64,772	416,344	946	2,474,785
Man	121,173	19,482	7,035	17,310	59,890	2,167	227,057
Sas	100,748	14,714	4,811	6,792	31,761	19	158,845
Al	355,173	44,102	35,184	10,821	108,464	267	554,009
BC	483,307	61,634	35,816	8,151	159,973	-	748,881
NWT	12,346	3,235	-	1,236	5,413	-	22,230
YU	1,811	732	-	504	2,988	-	6,035
Totals	4,441,399	465,507	297,081	159,502	1,234,977	3,670	6,602,136

1991-92 Due to the federal Government Expenditures Restraint Act, details of expenditures for payments to Ontario, Alberta and British Columbia aren't available.

Nfld	88,738	6,234	12,541	6,451	8,653	242	132,859
PEI	19,644	4,396	1,715	1,134	7,866	-	34,755
NS	143,891	20,593	8,435	9,374	33,787	1,643	217,723
NB	129,687	11,176	8,410	3,259	54,404	-	206,936
Que	1,418,044	227,539	106,784	36,036	428,900	642	2,217,945
Ont	-	-	-	-	-	-	2,158,851
Man	142,527	18,090	9,417	18,381	61,987	2,724	253,126
Sask	102,704	15,697	2,434	6,458	49,742	-	177,035
Alta	-	-	-	-	-	-	623,276
BC	-	-	-	-	-	-	747,342
NWT	11,508	4,818	-	1,626	5,822	-	23,774
Ykn	3,256	502	-	444	3,968	-	8,170
Total	n/a	n/a	n/a	n/a	n/a		6,801,792

In 1990-91, payments to Ontario are indicated on the line starting "On", ending with the amount of 2,474,785. This amount was adjusted in 1991-92 for an overpayment recovered by the federal government, resulting from the federal Government Expenditures Restraint Act.

1992-93 ($000)Due to the federal Government Expenditures Restraint Act, details of expenditures for payments to Ontario, Alberta and British Columbia aren't available.

Provnc	Genrl Assist	Hms SpcCr	Hlth Care	Child Welf.	Welf Serv. Prjs	Wrk Actv	Totals
Nfld	98,421	7,059	15,218	6,897	23,694	109	151,398
PEI	21,373	4,034	1,547	884	7,653	-	35,491
NS	170,075	19,261	11,082	12,547	33,759	1,887	248,611
NB	154,296	9,275	8,335	3,220	52,187	-	227,313
Que	1,602,256	214,704	132,710	39,591	496,572	386	2,486,219
Ont	-	-	-	-	-	-	2,282,903
Man	172,470	18,427	8,425	20,247	72,792	1,872	294,233
Sask	124,813	17,386	6,987	8,042	39,821	-	197,049
Alta	-	-	-	-	-	-	618,960
BC	-	-	-	-	-	-	803,204
NWT	15,732	3,178	-	1,311	6,097	-	26,318
Ykn	4,220	1,238	-	271	5,225	-	10,954
Total	n/a	n/a	n/a	n/a	n/a		7,382,653

1993-94

	Genrl Assist	Hms SpcCr	Hlth Care	Child Welf.	Welf Serv. Prjs	Wrk Actv	Totals
Nfld	109,607	6,561	22,191	8,618	26,599	-	173,576
PEI	22,795	4,006	1,667	891	8,097	-	37,456
NS	182,899	20,193	11,281	14,302	34,868	976	264,519
NB	142,481	9,556	8,249	6,025	42,225	-	208,536
Que	1,742,674	211,457	154,184	42,844	523,955	196	2,675,310
Ont	-	-	-	-	-	-	2,520,716
Man	178,166	14,264	8,199	26,872	78,204	1,261	306,966
Sask	145,530	19,566	8,240	8,510	45,515		227,361
Alta	-	-	-	-	-	-	587,924
BC	-	-	-	-	-	-	839,549
NWT	17,192	3,112	-	1,628	6,557	-	28,489
Ykn	4,876	1,658	-	(1,621)	5,260	-	10,173
Totals	n/a	n/a	n/a	n/a	n/a		7,880,571

1994-95 & 1995-96, the two final years are not yet available

The following totals are from the above federal payments data. No totals by programs are available for years after 1991 due to the Federal Government Restraints Act as noted above. Provincial share of costs aren't included here.

TOTAL FEDERAL PAYMENTS BY PROGRAMS, BY YEARS

PROGRAMS	1982-83 ($000)	1983-84 ($000)	1984-85 ($000)	1985-86 ($000)	1986-87 ($000)
Genrl Assist	2,082,536	2,470,860	2,760,944	2,940,204	3,061,990
Hm SpcCr	384,324	389,719	396,711	394,242	316,838
Hlth Care	70,423	97,291	109,959	153,542	171,357
Child Welf	174,257	174,205	135,467	123,019	104,613
Welf Serv	473,786	505,303	594,309	668,263	779,658
WkAc Prjs	5,098	5,523	3,101	4,309	3,935
Totals	3,190,424	3,642,901	4,000,551	4,283,579	4,438,391

PROGRAMS	1987-88 ($000)	1988-89 ($000)	1989-90 ($000)	1990-91 ($000)
Genrl Assist	3,196,963	3,393,158	3,573,159	4,441,399
Hms Spsc	364,481	427,201	423,427	465,507
Hlth Care	194,468	212,162	243,989	297,081
Chld Welf	124,560	156,894	135,408	159,502
Welf Serv	841,912	914,072	1,121,972	1,234,977
WkAc Prjcs	3,956	4,905	4,599	3,670
Totals	4,726,340	5,108,392	5,502,554	6,602,136

The above presentations of data begin in 1982-83 and end in 1993-94; prior years, and years subsequent to 1993-94 can be obtained from the catalogues of SOCIAL SECURITY STATISTICS (See FOOTNOTES) However, data of Welfare Services and Work Activity can't be gleaned from SOCIAL SECURITY STATISTICS, because they're not separated; also, Health Care data and "Notes" are unsettled in Table 2, and "Notes" are unsettled in Appendix A. And furthermore, years after 1990-91 aren't reported for 3 provinces, due to the Restraints Act. Most historical purposes wouldn't require the details of the above tables, except to approximately comprehend provincial differences by program components. Actually there are many more differences than here cited, and actual copies of the Annual Reports are necessary for more complete data comprehension. However, more complete comprehension of the data information is available concerning all sorts of intervening data variables. See catalogue "NOTES" of the SOCIAL SECURITY

STATISTICS. Printed catalogues of the "NOTES" and data are Cat.#s MP90-2/17-1993 & MP90-2/17-1995. Social Security Statistics data are on the internet to 1997; start at the National Site Home page, Human Resources Development, http://www.hrdc-drhc.gc.ca/

Descriptions and data information of the above presentation of trends was obtained from the CANADA ASSISTANCE PLAN Annual Reports which are published by Human Resources Development Canada. Reproductions are with the permission of the Minister of Public Works and Government Services Canada.

OTHER INFORMATION OF ANNUAL REPORTS, CANADA ASSISTANCE PLAN
Statistics from Annual Reports, CANADA ASSISTANCE PLAN.
The following formats and varieties of other information about the Canada Assistance Plan are available in Canada Assistance Plan Annual Reports year by year (see "FOOTNOTES" below).

Table 2:   Number of Persons Assisted under the Canada Assistance Plan, April to March each year, by Provinces and Territories.
Table 3:   Total Number of Homes for Special Care
Table 4:   Total Number of Provincially Approved Agencies
Table 5:   Total Number of Provincial Laws
Table 6:   Number of Persons Assisted, by years
Table 7:   Summary of Federal Payments to Provinces and Territories, by years
Table 8:   Federal Payments to Provinces and Territories 1985 to 1994[4]

Canada
Assistance
Plan

FOOTNOTES TO APPENDIX VI: ANNUAL REPORTS OF CANADA ASSISTANCE PLAN

1. CANADA ASSISTANCE PLAN ANNUAL REPORT(S), Published by authority Minister of Human Resources Development. p. 8. Copies of the reports are available from the Enquiries Centre, Human Resources Development Canada, 140 Promenade du Portage, Portage IV, Level 0, Hull, Quebec K1A 0J9

2. Ibid pp. 9-11.

3. Ibid pp. 20-etc

4. Ibid 1993-94, pp. 22 to 28

APPENDIX VII: SOCIAL SECURITY STATISTICS

These volumes are published by authority of the Minister of Human Resources Development - Government of Canada - and are available from the Minister of Supply and Services Canada.

Cat. No. MT90-2/17-1993, ISBN 0-662-61662-6,[1]
Cat. No. MP90-2/17-1995, ISBN O-662-62742-3[2]

The Introduction of the publications includes the statement, "The aim of this report is to provide an account of income security and social services expenditures in Canada, the number of beneficiaries for most of the programs, and the total social security program expenditures." p.10.

SOCIAL SECURITY STATISTICS are presented in Overview Tables 1 and 2 on pp. 12 to 23 of the 1968-69 to 1992-93 catalogue. (Overview Tables 1, 2 & 3 are in subsequent catalogues.)

Table 1 - Total Social Security Expenditures in Canada
1968-69 to 1992-93 p.13.[3]
1970-71 to 1994-95 p.13[4]
1972-73 to 1996-97-pending[5]

Table 1 utilizes socio economic data described in detail in Appendix C of the catalogues, regarding, Gross Domestic Product, Net National Income and Overall Government Expenditures. pp.12-13. Table 1 "Notes" explain that Total Government Expenditures are based on "Statistics Canada System of National Accounts" which haven't been referenced in our present study of A History of the CANADA ASSISTANCE PLAN. 1970-71 to 1994-95 catalogue Table 1 includes total education expenditures, for the first time, and bottom-line totals updated for all years are therefore different than in prior catalogues. The Canada Assistance Plan expenditures aren't specified but are included - in the Table 1 totals; and outlined in Table 2 as Tables 332 to 431; and detailed in Tables 332 to 434 of SOCIAL SECURITY STATISTICS.

SOCIAL SECURITY STATISTICS - APPENDIX A in the catalogues - Methodology in the Catalogues outlines sources from where the information was obtained.

The following statistics include expenditures from all levels of government - federal, provincial and municipal. As the catalogues explain, there are some limitations to the methodology of obtaining and recording the following statistics.

Complete 1968-69 to 1992-93 data, from the catalogue, aren't shown here. Table 1, in the 1968-69 to 1992-93 catalogue, shows expenditures, as calculated, including welfare + health = total of social security programs. (In Table 1 of the 1968-69 to 1992-93 catalogue, a different bottom-line doesn't account education costs of Canada's Social Security. Years 1973-74 to 1996-97 catalogues weren't available)[6]

Table 1 Total Social Security Expenditures in Canada 1970-71 to 1994-95, as calculated, include welfare + health + education = total of social security programs.[7]

Year Total	Gross Social Security Expenditures (current$) (000,000)	Total Domestic Product (GDP) $(000,000)	Per Capita Government Expenditures (Current dollars) $(000,000)	Per Capita Expenditure ($)
1994-95	199,165	760,487	363,932	6,809.50
1993-94	199,763	720,534	362,442	6,902.52
1992-93	196,364	694,563	357,564	6,879.78
1991-92	186,604	680,410	345,523	6,635.97
1990-91	167,742	670,744	323,371	6,035.91
1989-90	151,812	658,862	296,494	5,544.76
1988-89	140,869	618,101	271,900	5,237.78
1987-88	130,985	565,909	252,080	4,933.56
1986-87	122,534	513,956	236,554	4,676.18
1985-86	114,240	486,173	225,907	4,403.75
1984-85	105,527	452,992	210,939	4,105.82
1983-84	98,624	416,385	194,300	3,874.23
1982-83	91,027	379,193	177,675	3,611.91
1981-82	76,037	362,780	153,528	3,053.71
1980-81	66,383	321,225	130,410	2,699.24
1979-80	57,603	285,145	111,484	2,372.75
1978-79	53,047	249,124	99,445	2,206.95
1977-78	47,938	222,941	89,376	2,014.51
1976-77	42,283	203,457	79,447	1,797.94
1975-76	36,988	178,033	70,585	1,593.68
1974-75	30,165	156,895	58,951	1,318.71
1973-74	24,918	133,315	47,708	1,104.55
1972-73	21,996	112,665	41,068	987.06
1971-72	19,014	100,127	36,349	863.24
1970-71	16,916	90,251	32,120	794.29

The above data, with regard to expenditures, don't indicate revenues realized by some programs such as Canada Pension Plan, Employment Insurance, and for Workman's Compensation.

Programs of the Canada Assistance Plan didn't include all Social Security programs: Canada Assistance Plan programs were included among all other Social Security programs. Our concentration on A History of the CANADA ASSISTANCE PLAN in this study can't extend to all programs, years and details, but the catalogues of SOCIAL SECURITY STATISTICS include the following lists of Tables, of Canada Assistance Plan programs, and of non C.A.P. programs.

Canada Assistance Plan programs: List of Tables

360   Total Federal-Provincial Cost Shared Program Expenditures
361   Number of Beneficiaries of General Assistance
         (including dependants), as of March 31

362 Total Federal-Provincial Cost Shared Expenditures for General Assistance
412 Total Federal-Provincial Cost-shared Expenditures for Homes for Special Care for Adults
413 Total Federal-Provincial Cost-Shared Expenditures for Homes for Special Care for Adults Applied to the Year of Provincial Expenditure
414 Number of Beds in Homes for Special Care for Children, as of March 31, 1972 to 1993
415 Total Cost-Shared Expenditures for Homes for Special Care for Children
416 Total Federal-Provincial Cost-Shared Expenditures for Homes for Special Care for Children Applied to the Year of Provincial Expenditure
421 Number of Children in Care Under Cost-Shared Arrangements for Child Welfare
422 Total Federal-Provincial Cost Shared Expenditures for Child Welfare
423 Total Federal-Provincial Cost-Shared Expenditures for Homes for Child Welfare Applied to the Year of Provincial Expenditure
424 Total Federal-Provincial Cost-Shared Expenditures for Health Care
425 Total Federal-Provincial Cost-Shared Expenditures for Health Care Applied to the Year of Provincial Expenditure
431 Total Federal-Provincial Cost Shared Expenditures for Other Welfare Services and Work Activity
432 Total Federal-Provincial Cost Shared Expenditures for Other Welfare Services and Work Activity Applied to the Year of Provincial Expenditure
434 "Total Federal Payments".[8]

(See Chapter 2 and APPENDIX VI for more information regarding Canada Assistance Plan sources, and for quotes and footnotes of pertinent statistics)

Non CAP programs: List of Tables

The following tables are all other programs of SOCIAL SECURITY STATISTICS, in the same Catalogue as the above list of CAP tables for 1968-69 to 1992-93.

Family Allowances
111 Annual Average Number of Children Receiving Allowances
112 Annual Average Number of Families Receiving Allowances
113 Net Federal Payments"
"Youth Allowances and Quebec Schooling Allowances 1968-69 to 1973-74
114 Number of Youths Receiving Allowances, as of March 31
115 Federal Payments"

"Federal Child Tax Credit, Taxation Years 1978 to 1992
116 Number of Families Receiving Credit
117 Number of Children Eligible for Benefits Under the Program
118 Total Amount of Credits"

"Total Old Age Security Programs
120 Total Net Federal Payments

"Old Age Security
121 Annual Average Number of Beneficiaries
122 Net Federal Payments"

"Guaranteed Income Supplement
123 Annual Average Number of Beneficiaries
124 Net Federal Payments"

"Spouse's Allowance 1975-76 to 1992-93
125 Annual Average Number of Beneficiaries
126 Net Federal Payments"

"Federal Training and Employment Programs
131 National Training Program, Institutional Training,
     Number of Trainees Started, 1968-69 to 1984-85
132 National Training Program, Institutional Training,
     Federal Payments, 1968-69 to 1984-85
133 National Training Program, Industrial Training,
     Number of Trainees Started, 1971-72 to 1984-85
134 National Training Program, Industrial Training,
     Federal Payments, 1971-72 to 1984-85
135 Canadian Jobs Strategy, Total Number of Participants,
     1985-86 to 1991-92
136 Canadian Jobs Strategy, Total Expenditures, 1985-86 to 1991-92
137 Federal Employment Programs and Services, Total Number of Participants,
     1992-93
138 Federal Employment Programs and Services, Total Expenditures,
     1992-93

"Social Assistance and Social Services for Registered Indians On Crown Lands,
On and Off Reserves
141 Federal Expenditures for Social Assistance
142 Federal Expenditures for Social Services

"War Veterans and Civilian War Allowances
151 Number of Beneficiaries as of March 31
152 Federal Payments"

"Veterans and Civilians' Disibility Pensions
153 Number of Beneficiaries as of March 31
154 Federal Payments"

"Canada and Quebec Pension Plans
210 Total Payments (All Benefits)
211 Annual Average Number of Retirement Pension Beneficiaries 1970-71 to
     1992-93"
212 Payments to Retirement Benefit Beneficiaries

250   Total Payments

"Old Age Assistance, 1968-69 to 1969-70
321   Number of Beneficiaries as of March 31
322   Total Federal-Provincial Cost Shared Payments

"Blind Persons Allowances, 1968-69 to 1980-81
331   Number of Beneficiaries as of March 31
332   Total Federal-Provincial Cost Shared Payments

"Disabled Persons' Allowances, 1968-69 to 1980-81
341   Number of Beneficiaries as of March 31
342   Total Federal-Provincial Cost Shared Payments

"Unemployment Assistance
352   Total Federal-Provincial Cost Shared Payments"

Canada Assistance Plan Tables 360 to 434 are above.

"Vocational Rehabilitation of Disabled Persons
442   Total Federal-Provincial Cost Shared Payments"
"Provincial Tax Credit/Rebate Program 1972-73 to 1992-93
521   Payments"

"Provincial Welfare Program
522   Payments for Programs not Cost-Shared with the Federal Government"

"Municipal Welfare, Calendar Years 1968 to 1992
911   Net Expenditures".[9]

Tables for the subsequent catalogue of 1970-71 to 1994-95 include the same Tables as for 1968-69 to 1992-1993, except Tables 321 and 322 which became outdated. And, new Tables for 1970-71 to 1994-95 are Tables 105, 106 and 107.

"Child Tax Benefit
105   Annual Average Number of Children Receiving Benefits
106   Annual Average Number of Families Receiving Benefits
107   Total Benefits Paid".[10]

FOOTNOTES TO APPENDIX VII: SOCIAL SECURITY STATISTICS

1. SOCIAL SECURITY STATISTICS, CANADA AND PROVINCES, 1968-69 to 1992-93, published by authority of the Minister of Human Resources Development Canada, and is available from the Minister of Supply and Services Canada 1994. Cat. No. MT90-2/17-1993, ISBN 0-662-61662-6

2. SOCIAL SECURITY STATISTICS, CANADA AND PROVINCES, 1970-71 to 1994-95, published by authority of the Minister of Human Resources Development Canada, and is available from the Minister of Supply and Services Canada 1994. Cat. No. MP90-2/17-1995, ISBN 0-662-62742-3

3. SOCIAL SECURITY STATISTICS, CANADA AND PROVINCES, 1968-69 to 1992-93, CANADA ASSISTANCE PLAN pp. 6-8.

4. SOCIAL SECURITY STATISTICS, CANADA AND PROVINCES, 1970-71 to 1994-95

5. SOCIAL SECURITY STATISTICS, CANADA AND PROVINCES, 1972-73 to 1996-97. Printed catalogue not yet available.

6. Ibid - internet re 1973-74 to 1996-97. Social Security Statistics data are on the internet to 1997; start at the National Site Home page, Human Resources Development, http://www.hrdc-drhc.gc.ca/

7. SOCIAL SECURITY STATISTICS, CANADA AND PROVINCES, 1970-71 to 1994-95, published by authority of the Minister of Human Resources Development Canada, and is available from the Minister of Supply and Services Canada 1994. Cat. No. MP90-2/17-1995, ISBN 0-662-62742-3

8. SOCIAL SECURITY STATISTICS, CANADA AND PROVINCES, CANADA ASSISTANCE PLAN. Tables listed in the Catalogues including through 1970-71 to 1994-95.

9. SOCIAL SECURITY STATISTICS, CANADA AND PROVINCES, other programs (not Canada Assistance Plan programs) of the catalogues including through 1970-71 to 1994-95

10. SOCIAL SECURITY STATISTICS, CANADA AND PROVINCES, List of New Child Tax Credit Tables 1972-73 to 1994-95

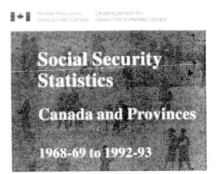

APPENDIX VIII: FINANCIAL DATA

PUBLIC ACCOUNTS OF CANADA[1]

BUDGETARY EXPENDITURE CLASSIFIED BY FUNCTION
Fiscal Years Ending March 31
"Millions of Dollars"
(Actually the data are in billions as six zeros
follow after each $ number, i.e. 000,000)

My comments here, about the Public Accounts of Canada, might appear to be critical of problems involved in record keeping of the Government of Canada, but the study here is involved with government information amidst ongoing dynamic, changing events of populations and records. And Canada's central government, whether by resources of records keeping, or by advanced public services know-how, excels all other Canadian governments. Minute by minute, in Canada, the central government co-ordinates all sorts of data, from all parts of Canada, about the people of Canada. Other governments of Canada rarely co-ordinate among each other about the peoples of the different provinces and territories. And within each province and territory, data information maintained by each government about peoples internal within their jurisdictions isn't comparable to the data information maintained by the central government about all people in Canada.

Yet, even in the central government, in time intervals, for examples, public administration dramatically changed, from 1970s to the 1980s to the 1990s, especially the contexts of budgetary problems. According to a reply to my enquiries about Public Accounts from the Coordination Division of Public Accounts, as of 1997, "Since the method of reporting budgetary expenditures changed over the years, this explains why it is often difficult to compare data from year to year. In the last 20 years, budgetary expenditures have been reported by function, activity, envelope, type, etc. The only information unfortunately available is the one reported in the Public Accounts."[1]

Some varying expenditures and incomes of the Government of Canada aren't included in this classification, (in specified fiscal years, excluded and included amounts are noted by Public Accounts); for example, expenditures excluded for the fiscal year 1983/84, "amounts charged to the Canada Pension Plan Account, the superannuation accounts, The Unemployment Insurance Account - except for benefits to fishermen, other specified purpose accounts and other liability accounts." (see Catalogue P51-1/1984-1E) From 1967 to 1976, Old Age Security payments weren't included in reports of Health and Welfare expenditures. (PUBLIC ACCOUNTS Cat.#BT 31-1 each year 1968 to 1970, and Cat.#P 51-1 each year 1971 to 1976)

From 1977 to 1985, Old Age Security payments were included in reports of Health and Welfare Expenditures (see Vol. 1, Cat.#P 51-1 each year). Auditors would review Public Account catalogues' notations for each year; where possible, source documents would be reviewed. As stated in Chapter 2, each column of data belongs to separate and different histories. The following expenditure records illustrate trends, not all expenditures. Some variables of recording expenditures are mentioned here above.

The following diagrams illustrate data in billions of dollars i.e. 000,000 after each $ number. (See footnote 1)

TOTAL BUDGETARY EXPENDITURES CLASSIFIED BY FUNCTIONS, COMPARED WITH HEALTH AND WELFARE FUNCTIONS.[2]

	TOTALS EXPENDED ALL FUNCTIONS*	HEALTH & WELFARE FUNCTIONS**	
1965	$ 7,218,000,000	$ 1,559,000,000	
1966	$ 7,659,000,000	$ 1,742,000,000	
1967	$ 8,718,000,000	$ 1,930,000,000	
1968	$ 9,798,000,000	$ 2,148,000,000	
1969	$ 10,738,000,000	$ 2,378,000,000	
1970	$ 11,921,000,000	$ 2,734,000,000	
1971	$ 13,182,000,000	$ 3,191,000,000	
1972	$ 14,841,000,000	$ 3,633,000,000	
1973	$ 18,645,000,000	$ 6,008,000,000	
1974	$ 22,839,000,000	$ 8,186,000,000	
1975	$ 29,213,000,000	$10,519,000,000	
1976	$ 33,978,000,000	$11,445,000,000	
1977	$ 39,011,000,000	$13,798,000,000	
1978	$ 42,902,000,000	$14,133,000,000	
1979	$ 46,923,000,000	$16,344,000,000	
1980	$ 53,422,000,000	$17,976,000,000	
1981	$ 62,297,000,000	$18,553,000,000	
1982	$ 74,873,000,000	$20,968,000,000	
1983	$ 88,521,000,000	$24,630,000,000	***
1984	$ 97,120,000,000	$28,604,000,000	***
1985	$109,628,000,000	$31,357,000,000	***

   * Sources: Total Net Government Budgetary Expenditures
  ** Sources: Total Health and Welfare Expenditures
 *** Sources: PUBLIC ACCOUNTS 1984-85

Public Account "Sources" include or exclude expenditures as noted above the illustration. In less than 10 years between 1965 and 1974, Health and Welfare expenditures in 1974 were greater than all 1965 expenditures of the Government of Canada. In 20 years between 1965 and 1985, yearly Health and Welfare Canada (HWC), total expenditures, (including all Health & Welfare Functions) advanced by a multiple of 20, mainly due to the introduction of Social Security programs. The following diagram includes data re Health and Welfare from the above diagram (See footnote 1)

	HEALTH & WELFARE FUNCTIONS (000)	CANADA ASSISTANCE PLAN (000)[3]
1966	$ 1,742,000,000	(pending)*
1967	$ 1,930,000,000	$ 10,500,000
1968	$ 2,148,000,000	$ 225,600,000
1969	$ 2,378,000,000	$ 257,855,000
1970	$ 2,734,000,000	$ 294,300,000
1971	$ 3,191,000,000	$ 391,643,000
1972	$ 3,633,000,000	$ 457,126,000
1973	$ 6,008,000,000	$ 477,600,000
1974	$ 8,186,000,000	$ 507,000,000
1975	$ 10,519,000,000	$ 901,000,000
1976	$ 11,445,000,000	$ 1,174,000,000
1977	$ 13,798,000,000	$ 1,379,000,000
1978	$ 14,133,000,000	$ 1,338,000,000
1979	$ 16,344,000,000	$ 1,465,000,000
1980	$ 17,976,000,000	$ 1,653,000,000
1981	$ 18,553,000,000	$ 1,941,000,000
1982	$ 20,968,000,000	$ 2,298,000,000
1983	$ 24,630,000,000	$ 2,832,000,000
1984	$ 28,604,000,000	$ 3,288,000,000
1985	$ 31,357,000,000	$ 3,745,000,000

* 1966 Canada Assistance Plan awaited legislated assent, pending claims & settlements of Categorical Programs which preceded CAP.

The above diagram extends data for Health and Welfare and for the Canada Assistance Plan, only from 1965 to 1985.

In the following diagram, data extends from 1965 to 1997, illustrating Canada Assistance Plan with total Public Accounts Expenditures for Canada. It should be stated again, histories in the illustrations of data information are separate and different for each column - see Chapter 2. But the C.A.P. data is included in the "PUBLIC ACCOUNTS TOTALS".

PUBLIC ACCOUNTS TOTALS EXPENDITURES ALL FUNCTIONS	PUBLIC ACCOUNTS RE FEDERAL C.A.P. EXPENDITURES IN CANADA**
1965 .... $ 7,218,000,000	....
1966 .... $ 7,659,000,000	....
1967 .... $ 8,718,000,000	.... $ 10,500,000
1968 .... $ 9,798,000,000	.... $ 225,600,000
1969 .... $ 10,738,000,000	.... $ 257,900,000
1970 .... $ 11,921,000,000	.... $ 294,300,000
1971 .... $ 13,182,000,000	.... $ 392,000,000
1972 .... $ 14,841,000,000	.... $ 457,000,000
1973 .... $ 18,645,000,000	.... $ 477,000,000
1974 .... $ 22,839,000,000	.... $ 507,000,000
1975 .... $ 29,213,000,000	.... $ 901,000,000
1976 .... $ 33,978,000,000	.... $ 1,174,000,000
1977 .... $ 39,011,000,000	.... $ 1,379,000,000
1978 .... $ 42,902,000,000	.... $ 1,338,000,000
1979 .... $ 46,923,000,000	.... $ 1,465,000,000
1980 .... $ 53,422,000,000	.... $ 1,653,000,000
1981 .... $ 62,297,000,000	.... $ 1,941,000,000
1982 .... $ 74,873,000,000	.... $ 2,298,000,000
1983 .... $ 88,521,000,000	.... $ 2,832,000,000
1984 .... $ 97,120,000,000	.... $ 3,288,000,000
1985 .... $109,628,000,000	.... $ 3,745,000,000
*1986 .... $111,528,000,000	.... $ 3,916,000,000
1987 .... $116,773,000,000	.... $ 4,051,000,000
1988 .... $125,406,000,000	.... $ 4,246,000,000
1989 .... $132,840,000,000	.... $ 4,556,000,000
1990 .... $142,637,000,000	.... $ 5,006,000,000
1991 .... $151,353,000,000	.... $ 5,788,000,000
1992 .... $156,389,000,000	.... $ 6,099,000,000
1993 .... $161,401,000,000	.... $ 6,686,000,000
1994 .... $157,996,000,000	.... $ 7,236,000,000
1995 .... $160,785,000,000	.... $ 7,266,000,000
1996 .... $158,918,000,000	.... $ 7,191,000,000
1997 .... $149,793,000,000	.... $ 105,000,000
1998 .... $149,684,000,000	.... $ 24,000,000[4]

*After 1985, PUBLIC ACCOUNTS of the Receiver General, Canada changed the format of reporting statistics from FUNCTIONS to ENVELOPES, and then to TYPES. The above illustration doesn't distinguish the different formats of "PUBLIC ACCOUNTS TOTALS" (See footnotes 1 & 2)

** Note: Data in the column, "PUBLIC ACCOUNTS RE FEDERAL C.A.P. EXPENDITURES", doesn't agree with the same data column reported in the volume titled, SOCIAL SECURITY STATISTICS by Human Resources Development Canada. According to Human Resources Canada, adjustments are going to be made.

My review and presentations of records of Public Accounts in no way intends to criticize nor to advise. My attentions have been cautiously transfixed on the growth of expenditures and debt, which were certainly not helter-skelter in records through 1966 to 1996, and the data   creates compelling effects. This isn't to say the research mesmerizes. On the contrary, research must be alert among deliberate, but certainly not contrived, growth in data of expenditures of PUBLIC ACCOUNTS. And records such as the following don't explain, nor comment about, long term growth of budgetary expenditures. Examples:

Long term expenditures' growth, per years 1965, 1985 & 1992.

1965	$ 7,218,000,000.00
1985	$ 109,628,000,000.00
1995	$160,785,000,000.00[5]

The following amounts illustrate growing billions of dollars adding onto growth each year in records of PUBLIC ACCOUNTS, regarding net debt growth from 1980 to 1992,

1980	$ 72,159,000,000.00	as of 88/89
1981	85,681,000,000.00	"
1982	100,553,000,000.00	"
1983	134,918,000,000.00	as of 91/92
1984	167,835,000,000.00	"
1985	206,347,000,000.00	"
1986	240,930,000,000.00	"
1987	271,633,000,000.00	"
1988	299,864,000,000.00	"
1989	328,815,000,000.00	"
1990	357,811,000,000.00	"
1991	388,429,000,000.00	"
1992	$ 423,072,000,000.00	as of 91/92[6]

See the GLOSSARY OF TERMS for definitions of "Debt" and "Deficits"

Here's the Debt from a STATEMENT OF ACCUMULATED DEFICIT[7]
(in millions of dollars i.e. 000,000 after each number)

	1986	1987	1988	1989	1990
Begin the year	207,986	242,581	273,32	3301,117	329,890
Year's Deficit	35,595	30,742	27,794	28,773	28,930
The year ends	242,581	273,323	301,117	329,890	358,820

	1991	1992	1993	1994	1995
Begin the year	358,820	390,820	425,177	466,198	508,210
Year's Deficit	32,000	34,357	41,021	42,012	37,462
The year ends	390,820	425,177	466,198	508,210	545,672

Explanations about growth in expenditures from 1965 to 1995, and growth of the debt from 1980 to 1992, should include economic analyses of such conditions as inflation, increases in wages and prices, and/or unemployment and stagflation, gross domestic product and net debt through the 1970s-80s. The research can't be analytically understood unless perhaps by economics analyses, including historical comments about all government program expenditures in the midst of the data information. A study such as this history of the Canada Assistance Plan cannot possibly approach such analysis. But pertinent historical information is supplied.

Management and organization theories aren't likely to bear more extensively upon 1980s and 1990s budgetary problems to find solutions. According to Douglas G. Hartle in 1989, "The time has come for an in depth assessment of the evaluation efforts of government with respect to the three Es of economy, efficiency and effectiveness. Such an assessment should, in my opinion, first and foremost be directed at the incentives under which elected and appointed officials carry out their responsibilities under a parliamentary system dominated by the competition for office among political parties."[8]

Evaluations of government are becoming more extensively studied and acted upon. A chapter concerning "The Policy Dimension of Public Administration, Implementing and Evaluating Public Policy" is included in the 1995 edition of PUBLIC ADMINISTRATION IN CANADA by Kernaghan and Siegel, with sub sections about "The Current State of Evaluations" and "Evaluating Evaluations".[9] And, the May 1996 Report of the Auditor General of Canada to the House of Commons includes Chapter 3 "Evaluation in the Federal Government"[10]

Everything stated above, regarding PUBLIC ACCOUNTS OF CANADA includes less than one half of all annual expenditures by federal, provincial and municipal governments in Canada. See APPENDIX VII, SOCIAL SECURITY STATISTICS, particularly Table 1 Catalogue "Notes" to Table 1 explain that Total Government Expenditures are based on "the Statistics Canada System of National Accounts".[11] This study of the CANADA ASSISTANCE PLAN hasn't referenced the System of National Accounts of Statistics Canada.

FOOTNOTES TO APPENDIX VIII - PUBLIC ACCOUNTS OF CANADA

1. Letter from Richard Deschenes, Manager, Public Account Coordination Division, Public Works and Government Services Canada, dated 5 August 1997.

2. PUBLIC ACCOUNTS OF CANADA, quoting Cat.#s, Volumes I & II & ISBN #s, charts or tables, by years 1966 to 1997, Minister of Public Works and Services, Canada. Most of the Cat.#s aren't by years of expenditures, because data quoted above, was updated in pertinent later years.

    Public Accounts, Vols.I of All Functions & HWC Functions
    1965   Cat.#BT31-1/1969-1, Chart p. 3.24
            ISBN# not applicable
    1966   Cat.#BT31-1/1970-1, Chart p. 3.24
            ISBN# n/a
    1967   Cat.#P51-1/1971-1, Table 3, p. 4.3
            ISBN# n/a
    1968   Cat.#P51-1/1971-1, Table 3, p. 4.3
            ISBN# n/a
    1969   Cat.#P51-1/1973-1, Chart p. 4.3
            ISBN# n/a
    1970   Cat.#P51-1/1974-1, Chart p. 4.3
            ISBN# n/a
    1971   Cat.#P51-1/1975-1, Chart 5A, p. 5.3
            ISBN# n/a
    1972   Cat.#P51-1,1976-1, Chart 6A, p. 6.4
            ISBN# n/a
    1973   Cat.#P51-1/1977-1, Table 2.3, p. 2.7
            ISBN#0-660-01477-1
    1974   Cat.#P51-1/1978-1, Table 1.3, p. 1.7
            ISBN#0-060-10117-3
    1975   Cat.#P51-1/1979-1, p.5.4
            ISBN#0-660-10436-9
    1976   Cat.#P51-1/1980-1E, p.5.4
            ISBN#0-660-10703-1
    1977   Cat.#P51-1/1981-1E, p.5.4
            ISBN#0-660-11011-3,
    1978   Cat.#P51-1/1982-1E, p.6.4
            ISBN#0-660-11193-4
    1979   Cat.#P51-1/1983-1E, p.6.2
            ISBN#0-660-11475-5
    1980   Cat.#P51-1/1989-1E, Table 1.8, p. 1.8
            ISBN#0-660-13335-0
    1981   Cat.#P51-1/1989-1E, Table 1.8, p. 1.8
            ISBN#0-660-13335-0
    1982   Cat.#P51-1/1989-1E, Table 1.8, p. 1.8
            ISBN#0-660-13335-0
    1983   Cat.#P51-1/1989-1E, Table 1.8, p. 1.8
            ISBN#0-660-13335-0
    1984   Cat.#P51-1/1993-1E, Table 1.3, p. 1.8
            ISBN#0-660-15361-0
    1985   Cat.#P51-1/1993-1E, Table 1.3, p. 1.8
            ISBN#0-660-15361-0

1986	Cat.#P51-1/1995-1E, Table 2.3, p. 2.4
	ISBN#0-660-16245-8
1987	Cat.#P51-1/1996-1E, Table 2.3, p. 2.4
	ISBN#0-660-16629-1
1988	Cat.#P51-1/1997-1E, Table 2.3, p. 2.4
	ISBN#0-660-16629-1
1989	Cat.#P51-1/1997-1E, Table 2.3, p. 2.4
	ISBN#0-660-16629-1
1990	Cat.#P51-1/1997-1E, Table 2.3, p. 2.4
	ISBN#0-660-16629-1
1991	Cat.#P51-1/1997-1E, Table 2.3, p. 2.4
	ISBN#0-660-16629-1
1992	Cat.#P51-1/1997-1E, Table 2.3, p. 2.4
	ISBN#0-660-16629-1
1993	Cat.#P51-1/1997-1E, Table 2.3, p. 2.4
	ISBN#0-660-16629-1
1994	Cat.#P51-1/1997-1E, Table 2.3, p. 2.4
	ISBN#0-660-16629-1
1995	Cat.#P51-1/1997-1E, Table 2.3, p. 2.4
	ISBN#0-660-16629-1
1996	Cat.#P51-1/1997-1E, Table 2.3, p. 2.4
	ISBN#0-660-16629-1
1997	Cat.#P51-1/1997-1E, Table 2.3, p. 2.4
	ISBN#0-660-16629-1

3. Ibid PUBLIC ACCOUNTS, Volumes I & II re HWC & C.A.P.

1967	Cat.#BT31-1/1968-2, Vol.II, Table 47, p. 3.49
	ISBN# not applicable
1968	Cat.#BT31-1/1969-1, Vol.I, Table 46, p. 3.50
	ISBN# not applicable
1969	Cat.#BT31-1/1970-1, Vol.I, Table 41, p. 3.45
	ISBN# n/a
1970	Cat.#P51-1/1971-2, Vol.II, p.15
	ISBN# n/a
1971	Cat.#P51-1/1971-2, Vol.II, p.15.13
	ISBN# n/a
1972	Cat.#P51-1,1976-2, Vol.II, p.15.10
	ISBN# n/a
1973	Cat.#P51-1/1977-1, Vol.I, Table 2.3, p. 2.7
	ISBN#0-660-01477-1
1974	Cat.#P51-1/1978-1, Vol.I, Table 1.3, p. 1.7
	ISBN#0-060-10117-3
1975	Cat.#P51-1/1979-1, Vol.I, Table 1.3, p. 1.7
	ISBN#0-660-10436-9
1976	Cat.#P51-1/1979-1, Vol.I, Table 1.3, p. 1.8
	ISBN#0-660-10436-9
1977	Cat.#P51-1/1981-1E, Vol.I, Table 1.3, p. 1.8
	ISBN#0-660-11011-3
1978	Cat.#P51-1/1981-1E, Vol.I, Table 1.3, p. 1.8
	ISBN#0-660-11011-3
1979	Cat.#P51-1/1981-1E, Vol.I, Table 1.3, p. 1.8
	ISBN#0-660-11011-3

1980	Cat.#P51-1/1989-1E, Vol.I, Table1.7, p. 1.7
	ISBN#0-660-13335-0
1981	Cat.#P51-1/1989-1E, Vol.I, Table1.7, p. 1.7
	ISBN#0-660-13335-0
1982	Cat.#P51-1/1989-1E, Vol.I, Table1.7, p. 1.7
	ISBN#0-660-13335-0
1983	Cat.#P51-1/1989-1E, Vol.I, Table1.7, p. 1.7
	ISBN#0-660-13335-0
1984	Cat.#P51-1/1993-1E, Vol.1, Table 1.3, p. 1-18
	ISBN#0-660-15361-0
1985	Cat.#P51-1/1993-1E, Vol.1, Table 1.3, p. 1-18
	ISBN#0-660-15361-0
1986	Cat.#P51-1/1995-1E, Vol.1, Table 2.3, p. 2.4
	ISBN#0-660-16245-8
1987	Cat.#P51-1/1996-1E, Vol.1, Table 2.3, p. 2.4
	ISBN#0-660-16629-1
1988	Cat.#P51-1/1997-1E Vol.1, Table 2.3, 2.3a, p. 2.4
	ISBN#-660-16629-1
1989	Cat.#P51-1/1997-1E "
	ISBN#-660-16629-1
1990	Cat.#P51-1/1997-1E "
	ISBN#-660-16629-1
1991	Cat.#P51-1/1997-1E "
	ISBN#-660-16629-1
1992	Cat.#P51-1/1997-1E "
	ISBN#-660-16629-1
1993	Cat.#P51-1/1997-1E "
	ISBN#-660-16629-1
1994	Cat.#P51-1/1997-1E Vol.1 Tables 2.3, 2.3a, p. 2.4
	ISBN#-660-16629-1
1995	Cat.#P51-1/1997-1E Vol.1 Tables 2.3, 2.3a, p. 2.4
	ISBN#-660-16629-1
1996	Cat.#P51-1/1997-1E Vol.1 Tables 2.3, 2.3a, p. 2.4
	ISBN#-660-16629-1
1997	Cat.#P51-1/1997-1E Vol.1 Tables 2.3, 2.3a, p. 2.4
	ISBN#-660-16629-1
1998	Cat.#P51-1/1998-1E Vol.1 Tables 2.3, 2.3a, p. 2.4
	ISBN 0-660-17656-4

4. Ibid ALL FED. EXPENDITURES compared with C.A.P. 1966-1998

5. PUBLIC ACCOUNTS, CANADA Expenditures growth, Fiscal Years Ended March 31 each year (Volume 1) 1965, 1985 & 1995.

6. Ibid re Debt (for 1980 to 1992, updated in 1989 and 1992)

7. GOVERNMENT OF CANADA PUBLIC ACCOUNTS PRESENTATION STATEMENT OF ACCUMULATED DEFICIT Catalogue #P51-111995-1E Volume I, TABLE 2.4, p. 2.4

8. CANADIAN PUBLIC ADMINISTRATION, "Perceptions of the Expenditure Budget Process" by Douglas G. Hartle, The Journal of the Institute of Public Administration of Canada, Fall 1989, Volume 32, Number 3. pp. 427-448.

9. PUBLIC ADMINISTRATION IN CANADA, A TEXT, Third Edition by Kenneth Kernaghan and David Siegel, published by Nelson Publications, Toronto, 1995, ISBN 0-17-604187-7

10. REPORT OF THE AUDITOR GENERAL OF CANADA TO THE HOUSE OF COMMONS, Chapter 3, "Evaluation in the Federal Govermnment" Minister of Public Works and Government   Services Canada 1996, Cat. No. FA1-1996/1-3E, ISBN 0-662-24468-0

11. SOCIAL SECURITY STATISTICS, CANADA AND PROVINCES, 1968-69 TO 1992-93, published by authority of the Minister of Human Resources Development Canada, 1994, p. 12, Cat. No. MT90-2/17-1993, ISBN 0-662-61662-6 (1970-71 to 1994-95 Cat. No. MP90-2/17-1995, ISBN 0-662-62742-3)

APPENDIX IX: FINANCIAL DATA

PUBLIC ACCOUNTS OF ONTARIO
(contents of columns a,b,c,d are described below)
NOTE: Following footnotes 2 & 4 reference federal documents.

a. Years	b. NET EXPENDITURES OF ONT. PROGRAMS [1]	c. SOCIAL SERVICES C.A.P. SHARED IN ONTARIO [2]	d. ONTARIO SOC SERV INCLUDE PROGRAMS NOT CAP SHARED[3]
1967	$1,799,121,181.39		$90,872,535.41
1968	2,296,619,235.50		$103,351,651.72
1969	2,775,204,293.71	$236,607,000.00	125,176,496,53
1970	3,249,244,180.68	263,678,000.00	130,617,729.80
1971	3,845,996,565.00	352,326,000.00	144,033,420.00
1972	5,223,004,022.00	422,070,000.00*	383,758,769.00
1973	6,480,342,060.00	420,982,000.00	420,257,333.00
1974	7,301,861,699.00	414,544,000.00	464,499,001.00
1975	8,821,609,717.00	567,416,000.00	674,094,578.00
1976	$10,632,241,331.00	789,158,000.00	881,473,684.00
1977	11,921,237,211.00	848,382,000.00	947,097,501.00
1978	13,129,483,713.00	823,052,000.00	$1,115,958,446.00
1979	14,156,942,763.00	870,594,000.00	1,225,737,460.00
1980	15,345,865,505.00	976,712,000.00	1,341,496.138.00
1981	16,835,819,882.00	$1,098,997,000.00	1,528,462,166.00
1982	19,651,000,000.00	1,266,456,000.00	1,770,000,000.00
1983	22,509,000,000.00	1,515,983,000.00	2,123,000,000.00
1984	24,553,177,408.00	1,700,436,000.00	2,401,898,627.00
1985	26,431,000,000.00	1,924,445,000.00	2,604,000,000.00
1986	32,460,000,000.00	2,104,717,000.00	2,863,000,000.00
1987	32,177,905,033.00	2,264,417,000.00	3,284,813,545.00
1988	34,941,856,174.00	2,646,186,000.00	3,774,742,482.00
1989	38,735,000,000.00	3,021,941,000.00	4,311,000,000.00
1990	41,602,000,000.00	3,522,964,000.00	5,062,000,000.00
1991	46,458,000,000.00	4,949,571,000.00	6,442,000,000.00
1992	51,683,000,000.00	4,317,702,000.00	8,314,000,000.00
1993	53,707,000,000.00	4,565,806,000.00	9,413,000,000.00
1994	53,883,438,100.00	5,041,432,000.00	9,166,886,808.00
1995	53,616,791,703.00	5,152,476,000.00	9,338,497,544.00
1996	58,155,099,816.00		8,919,940,533.00
1997	56,355,000,000.00		8,081,000,000.00
1998	56,454,000,000.00		8,080,000,000.00

PUBLIC ACCOUNTS OF ONTARIO cont'd
(notes re columns e & f on p. 126)

Years	e. FED. TRANSFERS TO ONTARIO RE CANADA ASSTNC.PLAN[4]	f. ALL ONTARIO SOC SERV INCLUDING PROGRAMS NOT C.A.P SHARED[5]	
1966			
1967		$90,872,535.41	
1968		$103,351,651.72	
1969	$118,304,000.	125,176,496,53	
1970	131,839,000.	130,617,729.80	
1971	176,163,000.	144,033,420.00	
1972	211,035,000.	383,758,769.00	
1973	210,491,000.	420,257,333.00	*
1974	207,272,000.	464,499,001.00	*
1975	283,708,000.	674,094,578.00	**
1976	394,579,000.	881,473,684.00	**
1977	424,191,000.	947,097,501.00	*
1978	411,526,000.	$1,115,958,446.00	
1979	435,297,000.	1,225,737,460.00	**
1980	488,356,000.	1,341,496.138.00	**
1981	549,499,000.	1,528,462,166.00	**
1982	633,228,000.	1,770,000,000.00	**
1983	757,992,000.	2,123,000,000.00	**
1984	850,218,000.	2,401,898,627.00	***
1985	962,223,000.	2,604,000,000.00	**
1986	$1,052,358,000.	2,863,000,000.00	**
1987	1,132,209,000.	3,284,813,545.00	
1988	1,323,093,000.	3,774,742,482.00	***
1989	1,510,970,000.	4,311,000,000.00	
1990	1,761,482,000.	5,062,000,000.00	
1991	2,474,786,000.	6,442,000,000.00	
1992	2,158,851,000.	8,314,000,000.00	
1993	2,282,903,000.	9,413,000,000.00	
1994	2,520,716,000.	9,166,886,808.00	***
1995	2,576,238,000.	9,338,497,544.00	***
1996	2,507,574,000. 6	8,919,940,533.00	***
1997		8,081,000,000.00	
1998		8,080,000,000.00	

* As of 1972, Ministry of Community and Social Services
a. Years shown in Ontario's Public Account Documents
b. Ontario Expenditures for all Programs, including C.A.P..
    And including provincial payments into municipal C.A.P.
    Shared Programs - see APPENDIX X example re Metro Toronto
c. Expenditures by Ontario on C.A.P., re Federal-Provincial Cost-Shared
    Program Expenditures. During final years, from 1990-1991 to 1996,
    federal payments were less than 50% for C.A.P. programs under the
    Federal Government Expenditures Restraint Act, re Ont., Alb., and B.C.
d. Ontario Expenditures for all Social Services Programs.

But programs such as Nursing Homes and Homes for Aged weren't shared by C.A.P.. Unexplained amounts in Column d. are incongruous for years 1969 to 1973, because all d. column years, including years 1969 to 1973, should show greater amounts than c. column, comparing years.

e. is data from SOCIAL SECURITY STATISTICS, CANADA
f. is from PUBLIC ACCOUNTS OF ONTARIO
    Incongruities are in columns e. & f. for years 1969-1973.

  * From Statement of Consolidated Revenue Fund
 ** Shown as in "Statement(s) of Budgetary Expenditures"
*** Summary of Budgetary Expenditures by Standard Accounts

Notes *, ** ,*** indicate different ACCOUNTS. See footnote #1 for descriptive headings of accounts over the years. Data Information was reported in several formats in former years, some of which formats have been changed. Reports continue to be reported in several formats in Ontario's Public Accounts. Sources of data used in this study can be tracked in particular years of the PUBLIC ACCOUNTS. Amounts of pertinent ACCOUNTS don't differ greatly within each particular year, except when ACCOUNTS are split, such as when Standard Objects were divided into Operating data and Capital data. In some jurisdictions, as in Metro Toronto, dividing Operating and Capital ACCOUNTS is often done. Capital costs were never shareable with the Canada Assistance Plan, except costs for some "Items of Special Need"; also computers and supplies were shareable, but other office supplies weren't. However, all such divided data aren't accounted in this history. Such data differences, where non-shareable office expenditures are included, don't greatly affect analysis of overall trends, although cost reviews, accounting and auditing would be greatly affected.

FOOTNOTES TO APPENDIX IX: PUBLIC ACCOUNTS OF ONTARIO

1. PUBLIC ACCOUNTS OF THE PROVINCE OF ONTARIO, for the Fiscal Years ended 31 March 1967-1997, described variably as "STATEMENT OF ORDINARY EXPENDITURE", "STATEMENT OF NET GENERAL EXPENDITURE" "STATEMENT OF EXPENDITURE BY PROGRAM", "SUMMARY OF BUDGETARY EXPENDITURE BY STANDARD ACCOUNTS", "SUMMARY OF BUDGETARY EXPENDITURE", STATEMENT OF EXPENDITURE". As found in the following volumes.
   - 1968-69 to 1970-71, Sessional Paper No. 1, Printed and Published by the Queen's Printer.
   - 1971-72 to 1976-77, Vol. 1 FINANCIAL STATEMENTS, Published by the Ministry of Treasury, Economics and Intergovernmental Affairs, Printed by the Queen's Printer
   - 1977-78 to 1985-86, Vol. 1, FINANCIAL STATEMENTS, Published by the Ministry of Treasury and Economics, Printed by the Queen's Printer.
   - 1986-87 to 1991-92, PUBLIC ACCOUNTS OF ONTARIO, Published by the Ministry of Treasury and Economics, (c) Queen's Printer ISSN 0381-2375.
   - 1991-92 to 1997-1998, PUBLIC ACCOUNTS OF ONTARIO, Vol. 2, Financial Statements, Published by Ministry of Finance, (c) Queen's Printer ISSN 0381-2375. (p.34 in 1997/98)

2. SOCIAL SECURITY STATISTICS, CANADA AND PROVINCES, 1968-69 TO 1992-93, and 1970-71 to 1994-95 published by authority of the Minister of Human Resources, Canada. Development Canada, and is available from the Minister of Supply and Services Canada 1994.
   Cat. No. MT90-2/17-1993, ISBN 0-662-61662-6
   Cat. No. MP90-2/17-1995, ISBN 0-662-62742-31.

3. PUBLIC ACCOUNTS OF THE PROVINCE OF ONTARIO, as above 1.

4. SOCIAL SECURITY STATISTICS, CANADA AND PROVINCES, see 2.

5. PUBLIC ACCOUNTS OF THE PROVINCE OF ONTARIO, see 1.

6. SOCIAL SECURITY STATISTICS, CANADA AND PROVINCES 1973-74 to 1996-97 data are on internet - start at National Site, Human Resources Development http://www.hrde-drhc.gc.cal and link to table 434

APPENDIX X: FINANCIAL DATA - TORONTO ANNUAL ESTIMATES

OPERATING PLAN AND BUDGET AS APPROVED BY METRO COUNCIL
(Metro budget data are variably reported as "estimates"
and "actuals", and "gross" is sometimes also "net")

METRO TORONTO EXPENDITURES

	GROSS METRO* ALL FUNCTIONS		COMMUNITY** and SOCIAL SERVICES,		PROVINCIAL GRANTS FOR SOCIAL SERVICES
1966	$ 221,674,929		$ 6,752,067	(a)	
1967	$ 389,693,479		$ 25,185,429		$ 13,142,647
1968	$ 428,998,173		$ 32,620,739		$ 18,855,644
1969	$ 472,627,985		$ 35,492,654		$ 20,243,198
1970	$ 542,439,024		$ 50,597,174		$ 30,066,604
1971	$ 563,721,458		$ 67,030,013		$ 41,306,014
1972	$ 473,056,700		$ 79,746,216		$ 54,219,623
1973	$ 470,886,141		$ 78,008,962		$ 51,161,994
1974	$ 198,500,570	(b)	$ 89,709,204		$ 58,460,351
1975	$ 230,808,600	(b)	$ 101,156,700		$ 70,797,000
1976	$ 716,067,302		$ 119,576,300		$ 85,891,800
1977	$ 834,522,068		$ 132,859,200		$ 96,226,000
1978	$ 901,885,268		$ 147,028,700		$ 106,359,000
1979	$ 984,703,005		unavailable re MIS ***		$ 112,658,600
1980	$1,060,496,694		$ 177,415,300		$ 128,839,600
1981	$1,183,167,816		$ 182,607,300	**** (c)	$ 140,283,700
1982	$1,376,379,029		$ 220,335,700	****	$ 168,748,000
1983	$1,521,208,082		$ 291,666,900	****	$ 225,801,100
1984	$1,660,385,750		$ 333,809,100	****(c)	$ 268,883,100
1985	$1,799,167,429		$ 336,178,300		$ 261,043,100
1986	$1,958,448,299		$ 377,221,700	est (c)	$ 288,221,800
1987			$ 560,381,200	****	$ 463,722,900
1988	$2,120,953,683		$ 647,417,000	actual	$ 402,436,700
1989	$2,051,167,200		$ 765,931,000	est.	$ 644,316,000
1990	$2,432,891.600		$ 935,705,000	****(c)	$ 763,992,900
1991	$2,916,824.900		$ 1,165,881,900	****	$ 933,977,500
1992	$3,201,917.900		$ 1,498,889,000	****	$ 1,248,126,000
1993	$3,429,146.400		$ 1,700,511,600		$ 1,332,686,000
1994	$3,452,600,700		$ 1,653,252,800	****	$ 1,393,067,000
1995	$3,457,160.000		$ 1,809,416,000	****	$ 1,559,322,000
1996	$3,121,927.000		$ 1,484,527,000	****	$ 1,072,852,000
1997	$3,122,589.000				$ 1,145,174,000

(a) 1966-1968 WELFARE DEPARTMENT, then subsequently became SOCIAL SERVICES DEPARTMENT, and lastly COMMUNITY and SOCIAL SERVICES (to 1997)

(b) Education costs not included

(c) CAS's not included

"PROVINCIAL GRANTS" reduce the above Community and Social Services costs of pertinent years, and consequently reduce Metro's gross costs. In other words, the above costs for Metro's "COMMUNITY and SOCIAL SERVICES" were shared between Metro and the Province. Shareable Provincial costs were shared with the Federal Government by way of the Canada Assistance Plan. (some costs weren't shareable under C.A.P.)

* Metro Gross Expenditures cover all costs for Protective Services, Transport, Environment, Recreation and Culture, Ambulance and General Government and shareable Metro Social Services, inclusive of capital financing charges.

** Community Services of Metro include costs which weren't shareable with Canada Assistance Plan for Homes for the Aged & Public Housing. Recoveries in those accounts are not recorded here. However, some recoveries channeled from Provincial Benefits and allowances toward Homes for the Aged and Public Housing were C.A.P. shareable. Those allowances and benefits in payments to recipients of Ontario Benefits etc. are included in data of Ontario Public Accounts. Under C.A.P. cost-sharing agreements, client records of Metro's allowances and Ontario's Family Benefits etc., were confidential.

*** not recorded as Metro was establishing MIS in 1979

**** Data above for years 1981 onward isn't continuous with all the other years, but other records at Metro do supply the years 1981 onward in other formats.

Metropolitan Toronto doesn't publish historical, data information reports. Metro does publish budgets. Some data is here presented from variable formats, and some data from estimates where actuals weren't available; all such data are sufficiently significant in this illustration of trends.

A History of THE CANADA ASSISTANCE PLAN isn't an audit. The data shown here is however accurate and verifiable from published Metro records, illustrated here historically by years, although there are format differences and differences between actuals and estimates in the data.

Some of the Metro Toronto data are quoted from estimates but most are actuals. See GLOSSARY OF TERMS for definitions of "estimates" & "actuals" & "trends" & "mill rates".

The following data information for selected years from 1975 to 1997, included in above, break down Community and Social Services costs for Hostels, Social Services and Children's Services, as compared again with Gross Metro Expenditures.

SELECTED YEARS	GROSS EXPENDITURES	METRO HOSTELS	SOCIAL SERVICES	CHILDREN'S SERVICES
1975	$ 230,808,600 (a)	$2,180.9	$54,537.3	$12,869.9
1976	716,067,302	2,538.5	58,854.9	14,213.8
1979	984,703,005	3,624.9	81,517.6	19,316.9
1980	$1,060,496,694	4,291.0	88,253.5	22,269.2
1982	1,376,379,029	7,880.4	$116,950.1	31,285.1
1983	1,521,208,082	$11,352.6	148,813.3	38,041.7
1984	1,660,385,750	12,777.4	158,529.2	42,080.8
1985	1,799,167,429	14,804.1	178,008.8	49,316.1
1986	1,958,448,299	17,589.3	207,764.9	61,237.9
1987				
1988	2,120,953,683	27,178.1	264,607.2	$106,459.7
1989	2,051,167,200	26,369.8	311,835.5	118,780.6
1990	2,432,891.600	26,936.1	465,886.9	135,529.6
1991	2,916,824.900	32,184.1	828,546.1	145,721.2
1992	3,201,917.900	37,886.8	$1,008,997.1	154,660.5
1993	3,429,146.400	41,775.1	1,199,534.0	170,450.8
1994	3,452,600,700	42,698.6	1,280,054.0	179,512.7
1995	3,457,160.000	48,878.0	1,238,382.0	182,827.0
1996	3,121,927.000	48,248.0	939,644.0	177,942.0
1997	3,122,589.000	51,973.0	905,453.0	187,748.0

(a) education costs not included

The following Provincial Grants were deducted from the above costs for Hostels, Social Services and Children's Services.

PROVINCIAL GRANTS TO METRO TORONTO

SELECTED YEARS	HOSTELS	SOCIAL SERVICES	CHILDREN'S SERVICES
1979	$2,775.3	$59,799.4	$15,779.1
1980	3,211.9	65,960.3	18,107.6
1982	6,017.2	87,088.3	25,745.2
1983	8,801.8	111,150.6	31.555.0
1984	$10,469.6	118,503.7	34,957.7
1985	12,212.5	133,271.0	40,707.9
1986	14,560.9	158,122.8	50,459.5
1987	19,431.4	184,947.2	67,511.2
1988	22,737.9	204,734.4	87,451.9
1990	21.671.0	368,216.0	94,867.8
1991	26,267.0	673,334.0	$108,468.0
1992	29,516.0	844,160.0	117,207.0
1993	33,807.0	$1,016,626.0	129,945.0
1994	34,463.0	1,089,762.0	134,577.0
1995	39,619.0	1,052,446.0	138,008.0
1996	37,538.0	771,206.0	127,200.0
1997	41,837.0	740,024.0	146,420.0

FOOTNOTE;- re APPENDIX X: Notes and notations are within this appendix. See furthur information in the ACKNOWLEDGEMENTS p. 178 re TORONTO ANNUAL ESTIMATES.

APPENDICES XI, XII, XIII, & XIV

HISTORICAL WRITINGS

APPENDIX XI

The following review/report paraphrases from NO FAULT OF THEIR OWN by James Struthers, University of Toronto Press, 1983, 268 pages.

Concepts about unemployment abounded in Canada before and after World War I. The most frequent excuse made by politicians, against giving relief, referred to the decline of agrarian, full employment. It was believed that relief spending wouldn't be necessary if the unemployed would go to work on farms. The argument was valid, on behalf of the farmers, from an historical point of view, but it didn't offer a rational argument on behalf of the unemployed.

Canadian politicians looked back to "full" employment of an agrarian Canada, and to Elizabethan Poor Laws which were needed in Britain's more urbanized society which provided for poor people if they were in their own parishes. (p. 6) "Full" employment existed in agrarian Canada through the 19th century when Britain's Poor Law Report of 1834 tightened up on Britain's unemployed who were considered to be 'less eligible' than independent labourers of the working class. Workhouse tests came into effect - relief was dispersed for forced labour inside central workhouses which were like penitentiaries. Britain's Poor Law assumed that examples of the harsh workhouses would motivate other labourers to find and to keep work rather than go to the workhouses.

Concepts In Canada about the Unemployed -
Cultural imperatives of enforcing the work ethic were as follows, here paraphrased-
----
"Less eligibility" quickly transferred to Canada. The author of NO FAULT OF THEIR OWN, James Struthers, believed that politicians and employers put the marketplace ahead of concerns for unemployed persons.

Employers and politicians argued that summer workers should save for wintertime layoffs.

It was believed there must be a wage rate at which full employment was feasible. Unemployed persons should accept lower wages to establish full employment

The problems of applicants for aid from charities were believed to be caused by thriftlessness, mismanagement, unemployment due to incompetence, intemperance, immorality, desertion of the family, and domestic quarrels. (p. 6)

Rural Canada was depopulating and immigrants were needed. It was therefore reasoned, as immigrants settled into rural life, if Canada needed immigrants to work in agriculture, no one should need relief. Unemployed immigrants, who needed relief, faced an unsympathic public. The Depressions of 1913 and 1930 coincided with high immigration in Canada. (pp.8-9)

'Back to the land' arguments -

- unemployment insurance was seen as unsuited - "Canada's recent industrialization before 1930 played a crucial role in limiting the subsequent response to mass unemployment in this country...the Depression was the 'first major collapse of the new urban-industrial Canadian economy'...the continuing strength of rural traditions in the country meant that Canadians going into the Depression shared a 'pioneer mentality' which viewed reliance on public relief as 'a confession of incompetence or sinfulness, of friendlessness and failure.' " (p. 210)

- the army of labourers for farmers and resource industries were provided with bunk houses and work; but the situations provided to the unemployed were humiliating, similar to the tasks required for poor relief at Toronto's House of Industry where it was required that a man wanting relief should break up a 650 lb crate of rocks.

What should be done? Who should do it?

The B.N.A. Act didn't have legislative sections which refer to the unemployed. "The constitution in the 1930s, as in the 1920s, provided more of a convenient excuse for delay than a barrier for action for both Bennett and King." (p. 209 - Bennett and King were Prime Ministers in Canada through the Depression)

There was a fear, after World War I, that jobless veterans might be more dangerous as unemployed men than were the unemployed men prior to the war. Veterans were provided with money and land.

Veteran's allowances ran out in 1920, and thereafter, the veterans were provided relief among other unemployed persons. Relief was funded by federal payments to municipalities equal to one-third the costs incurred by municipalities for relief of the unemployed - starting December 1920 - terminated in the spring of 1921 - resumed again in October 1921.

But these arrangements for relief payments were terminated altogether by the government of Mackenzie King 1922/23. (pp 27-29)

Bryce Stewart became Director of Employment Service of Canada 1918. He held the post until 1922.

"Stewart began his work as the first director of the Employment Service of Canada with a broad conception of its potential. To him, the ESC was 'only the first step in dealing with unemployment', part of a 'co-ordinated attack' that would have to include 'vocational guidance and technical education, regulation of private employment agencies, regulation of industry, systematic distribution of public employment, unemployment insurance' and a 'well thought out immigration policy' to prevent labour from 'being dumped on the market faster than it can be absorbed'. Above all, Stewart believed that 'too much stress cannot be laid on the importance of acquiring more and more information'. (p. 19)

Had Stewart's plans been put into effect, when he was director of the ESC, we might look back upon him as a genius, but governments began to cut back on funding of the Employment Service of Canada, and Stewart resigned in 1922. (p. 39)

By 1923, there were no more statistics being compiled about the incidence of unemployment. Even by 1930, in the ad hoc relief program, Ottawa didn't require registration of those who were provided with benefits - there was no way of knowing how many families and individuals were assisted.

1931-1932 the Depression reached its nadir as unemployment rose from 16% in August to 25% in February, and in 1933 it reached 30%.

A Social Worker is quoted, 'One meets some Workers of whom one thinks - "How old she looks! I never before thought of her as being old," noted Ethel Parker of Toronto's Neighbourhood Workers' Association...It was small wonder, 'many of us have grown a bit brittle and required "handling" as to our tempers. Can you see your cherished standards, one by one, go to the board; can your sympathies be torn day after day by tragedies of which most of the rest of the city remain unheeding; can you stand day after day in the position of being the only person to whom these families have to turn and yet be absolutely unable to relieve their anxiety and suffering?" (p. 50)

"To qualify for relief, families had to submit to humiliating means tests in order to prove that they were absolutely bereft of resources and that their relatives were unable to provide support. In most municipalities, driver's permits, licence plates and liquor permits, were confiscated. Bank deposits, insurance policies, and even possession of a telephone or radio could be grounds for disqualification..."In return for this complete surrender of their privacy, most families on the dole could expect to receive relief in the form of food vouchers, not cash, since it was generally conceded, even among social workers themselves, that without greater 'intensive supervision', relief in kind was far more 'effective and economical...for that percentage of those dependent on social aid, who cannot be entrusted safely with the freedom of cash relief.'" (p. 72)

NATIONAL EMPLOYMENT COMMISSION which began in 1931, reported in 1937 "recommendation that Ottawa assume total financial and administrative responsibility for the unemployed" - it was a watershed for the Canadian welfare state. Unemployment Assistance was also recommended, for those who would not be covered by unemployment insurance, but the principle of 'less eligibility' should be upheld. As far as possible, recipients should work for Aid received. (p. 176)

1938 grants in aid, as of January 1938, contained the stipulation that 'material Aid given to any family head or individual...must be less than the normal earning of any unskilled labourer.'

October to March, 1938/39, numbers on relief rose from 802,046 to 1,044,726. (p. 188)

The B.N.A. Act was amended 12 July 1940, in Britain, and became landmark legislation in Canada 1 August 1940, giving the federal government jurisdiction over unemployment insurance. And before the end of World War II, the federal government was preparing for an Unemployment Assistance program for unemployed persons who would not be covered by the insurance. (p. 202)

Rowell-Sirois Commission Report of the Royal Commission on Dominion-Provincial Relations recommended that the federal government should be responsible for relief and unemployment insurance. The principle of 'less eligibility' was upheld by Rowell-Sirois. (p. 204)

The writing of NO FAULT OF THEIR OWN implies, throughout the text, that abusive attitudes toward unemployed persons in Canada are realized and relegated to the past, but the very last page is truer to the reality about attitudes toward unemployed persons, "Once again economists, newspaper editors, and prime ministers have accused the unemployed of preferring relief to work...Welfare rolls have reached crisis proportions and mayors and premiers are again complaining that Ottawa is trying to 'shift the burden of unemployment to the provinces and municipalities.'" (p. 214)

APPENDIX XII

A PROPERLY SOCIALIZED SERVICE, Unemployment Relief and the Formation of Toronto's Civic Department of Welfare, a thesis by Alan Bass, 1989. - Graduate student. The thesis is on file at the Metropolitan Toronto Archives, 255 Spadina Road, Toronto.

The thesis tends to jump right into the Depression years without too much background about the government efforts in earlier years for the relief of needy persons.

Politicians in the City of Toronto had been focused on an economic expansion after World War I, and they were not very attentive to needy, unemployed persons. Welfare Relief was originally provided by the House of Industry in Toronto where food was distributed to needy persons.

Increasing demand for relief, 1929/30, created a crisis. The Department of Public Welfare was established in 1931, and the first Commissioner was Albert W. Laver. The function of the House of Industry was changed to provide Hostel services only. It would no longer distribute food. The Department of Public Welfare began to distribute food vouchers.

It seems that the Department of Public Welfare got very little attention from the City Council in the early years, but as the numbers of persons, who needed assistance, increased, the Commissioner was called upon to report to the Council. The Council was motivated by a policy of economy and control, and the department's Commissioner strictly followed the policy, but he also spoke out against the neglect of needy persons whenever extreme measures were suggested.

Hostel beds were provided at Seaton House, another hostel on Wellington Street, and another at the Exhibition Coliseum.

Other agencies involved in the relief of needy persons were the Board of Trade, Salvation Army, Y.W.C.A. and Y.M.C.A.

The persons who needed assistance increased by 10 times in subsequent years from 1930-1935. Alan Bass's thesis quotes from the Annual Report of the Commissioner of Finance, City of Toronto, 1942 - the following expenditures were reported regarding assistance to needy persons -

	Gross	Federal/ Provincial Share*
1930 welfare expenditure	$466,100.00	$88,530.00
1935 welfare expenditure	$9,983,508.00	$6,381,097.00
1940 welfare expenditure	$4,891,116.00	$3,700,814.00

* Administration costs were not shared, and the expenditures for the administration are not included here.

In January 1931, the Province of Ontario Department of Welfare issued guidelines to Toronto regarding the 2/3 rebate of funding for welfare assistance.

The Government of Ontario, called upon by municipalities across the province, where municipal finances had collapsed, became involved with welfare administration and assistance costs in the bankrupt municipalities. (This would seem to be the beginnings of arrangements which eventually became parts of the General Welfare Assistance Act for the funding by the province of the administration costs of municipal welfare. Actually, beginning in 1967, the administration expenditures were transferred to Claims on the Canada Assistance Plan for Welfare Services for federal contribution of 50%. In effect provincial costs, which the province shared 50% with municipalities, were totally paid by the federal government. Municipalities paid the other 50%)

APPENDIX XIII

DECADES OF SERVICE, A history of the Ontario Ministry of Community and Social Services, 1930-1980, by Clifford J. Williams, Copyright 1984, The Ministry of Community and Social Services, 134 pages, ISBN 0-7743-9004-2.

The history of the Ontario Ministry of Community and Social Services, by Clifford Williams, is similar to the histories THE GREAT DEPRESSION, by Pierre Berton, and NO FAULT OF THEIR OWN, by James Struthers. Whereas the texts by Berton and Struthers emphasize national histories, mainly about the Depression, Williams' Ontario history differs of course by a concentration on one province of Canada, with references to arrangements and agreements with the federal government. The substance of Clifford Williams' text outlines detailed particulars about politicians, committees, commissions, reports, protests, police actions, relief, public works, breaking rocks and unemployment. All these and many other particulars are mixed with contingent urges of early historical periods, followed by idealistic and rhetorical urges, all of which urges might be said to become established. My choice of wording to concisely describe the text and its substance is as difficult, I'm sure, as it was for Clifford Williams to research every particular of the history.

DECADES OF SERVICE certainly isn't an opening for complaints about faceless governments. It's a concentration on actual people who faced problems of "relief", welfare and social services for the periods through the years 1930-1980. The particulars in the text are presented in chapters, mainly about programs, chapters which go back to the beginnings of each program. Some programs began in the nineteenth century. The format of the text is probably most significant to people who work in each of the programs in time capsules apart from ongoing other programs. This surely can't be the way programs are viewed from the offices of the Minister, the Deputy Minister, and Area Managers of the Ministry of Community and Social Services, not to mention Commissioners and Managers of Municipal programs, and other concerned administrators who manage provincially approved programs. Yet in courses of time, all these too will meet with the outlined issues of this text.

The following Contents from the text covers the Chapters and other parts of DECADES OF SERVICE:

Author's preface

A message from the Minister

The presentation of the contents indicates the extent of the study and research involved in the composition of DECADES OF SERVICE. I've selected some quotations from Williams' text which are significant to my Concise Archival History of Social Services. The questions begged by these selected quotations can't be asked and answered here.

> "While there have been hot debates in the House and on the hustings and bitter criticisms and controversies over particular program aspects or proposed legislation, public welfare has been moulded from decade to decade much more by public beliefs and attitudes toward the poor or disadvantaged, by current notions as to dependency and government intervention and aid. The spirit of the time, popular morality, has been the guiding force, not the orthodox or eccentric ideas of right or left wing partisans. It is not strange that in a democracy party policy should express a high degree of coincidence with public

opinion." p. 46 (page numbers refer to pages in text of Decades of Service)

"An important lesson was learned. Where legal eligibility is based on objective, not moral or subjective considerations, personal knowledge of the applicant is unnecessary and, as often as not, a positive menace to his interests. Human contact for special services, such as counselling and investigation, could be maintained through a disinterested field staff. Appeals against unfavourable decisions, albeit through the same channels, could be made as often as the applicant persisted. The objectivity of the system was a guarantee of fairness, its simplicity a warrant of speed." p. 52

The author of DECADES OF SERVICE carries readers through a caldron of legislative quarrels and complaints, from which confusion, order emerged. In the midst of the rumblings, some services for children prevailed through the 1930s. Children's Corrections had been under public welfare jurisdiction of 5 industrial schools and 2 training schools.

David Croll had closed 2 industrial schools in favour of other services such as foster care homes. Training Schools cared for and supervised older, troubled children. Premier Hepburn transferred all the schools to the Provincial Secretary in 1937. Children's Corrections were returned to the Ministry of Community and Social Services in the 1970s. (This study doesn't mention provincial shared funding with the federal government for young offenders, which had been by way of the Social Services Division of Health and Welfare Canada, under the Young Offenders Agreement - the HWC connection was severed in the 1980s when funding arrangements went to the federal Solicitor General under the New Young Offenders Agreement.)

Troubled politicians and bureaucrats and administrators no doubt felt the distress of children in corrections services as much as did private agencies where programs were provided for children on probation, such as Y.M.C.A. clubs, and gym and swim programs. Should the distressed and rambunctious children be kept apart from the regular membership of children? Rationales among the staffs of private agencies were not unanimous in answers to the question.

A similar question about how to segregate distressed persons faced the oldest program in the Department. Quoting from page 55 of DECADES OF SERVICE,

"The oldest program in the Department's repetoire was the least regarded. These were "Refuges" of provincial reports, variously known to themselves as Houses of Providence, Houses of Industry, Homes for the Aged and Infirm, and Homes for the Friendless. In 1930 the new department had inherited the supervision and subsidy of seventy four refuges with a population of 5,272 "inmates"."

"The system had a history nearly a century long."

No sooner did municipalities recover responsibilities for budgeting their own programs, after the worst years of the Depression, councils were shocked to find in their midsts houses of refuge providing for all variety of indigent and unemployed persons,

> "A walk through drab and narrow corridors, through the cheerless wards jam packed with beds.... councillors who had seldom or never been in the refuge or only at the best of times, were usually appalled. More than one was nauseated by the odorous if not odious scene. They often decided on the spot that a great change must be made." p. 58.

By 1944 there were 10,000 people occupying much the same living space where 5,000 were living in 1930. The Minister, William Goodfellow, and the Deputy Minister James Band, readily accepted and shared a vision of an inspector of the refuges, Earl Ludlow, through whose efforts "Homes for the Aged were, in a few short years, on the statute books, expressing a generous provincial government policy that grew and blossomed for a generation". p. 58.

Earl Ludlow would in later years recall the living conditions he found in municipal refuges - "close packed wards, with bedrooms and halls filled with men and women of various ages: most of them very old, some helplessly retarded and scarcely out of childhood, people in every state of body and mind. The alert and sensitive aged had to live side by side with the helplessly senile and incontinent; the able bodied with the crippled; the bed ridden and ill with the healthy and the obstreperous; each disturbing and distressing the other with their different needs, complaints and behaviours; all thronged together in unsegregated closeness to live out the balance of their days. There was seldom enough elbow room, enough silence, enough attention, or enough access to common facilities for bathing, toileting, eating or sleeping." p. 57.

DECADES OF SERVICE doesn't outline the many provincial programs, which were non shareable under the Canada Assistance Plan, but were share funded from the federal government under health divisions of Health and Welfare Canada,* and by the Extended Program Financing Act of the federal government. CAP did share some costs, such as Items of Special Need, for residents of some health programs. Correctional services were all non shareable under CAP. (*the Canada Assistance Plan was administered by (HWC), the federal Department of Health and Welfare between 1966 and 1993. The federal Department of Human Resources Development, Canada took over the Canada Assistance Plan in 1993.)

Children's and institutional programs are compelling welfare concerns, but by far and away beyond the expenditures incurred by Children's programs, are costs for income maintenance programs. DECADES OF SERVICE outlines many historical features of Ontario's income maintenance programs. The categorical programs which were share funded by provincial and federal governments, before the present income maintenance programs in Ontario, could be dissolved when the Canada Assistance Plan was legislated.

> "A central feature of the Canada Assistance Plan was its generality. That is, all "persons in need" were eligible; they did not have to exhibit such other criteria as age or disability. The categorical allowances, Old Age Assistance, Blind and Disabled Persons Allowances, and even Mothers' Allowances, could be dissolved into one type of aid."

> "The Family Benefits Act, effective July 8, 1966, was the immediate response of the department to the Canada Assistance Plan. All income maintenance issued directly by the Province was gathered into this one piece of legislation. The short term cases remained under the General Welfare Assistance Act." p. 81

> "From 1950 to 1970, the municipalities participated in the unprecedented and unsurpassed progress achieved by the Department of Public Welfare. The municipalities seized opportunity after opportunity as it was offered to them through provincial legislation to introduce new services and to improve existing ones. Issuing general assistance remained their basic, indispensible function. Fortunately, the economy of the time was generally prosperous, though there were episodes of significant unemployment that strained municipal resources." p. 89

Case loads of Family Benefits and General Welfare Assistance increased greatly thereafter. Through the 1970s and into the 1980s, the case loads and costs of income maintenance accelerated at a disconcerting pace chased by the twin devils of mounting unemployment and inflation". p. 81.

Flashing back through the history of income maintenance, as presented in DECADES OF SERVICE,

- unemployment relief from the beginning of settlement of what is now Ontario. p. 13. (19th century described as times of full employment by NO FAULT OF THEIR OWN-see Appendix XI)
- Royal Commission on Public Welfare, under Philip D. Ross, 1930 report recognized a need for one department for various welfare programs. "Public welfare" in the 1920s was a concept not well defined, scarcely distinguishable among general notions of public health, physical and mental care and treatment, charitable aid, corrections and reform." p.2. "All...services which we now think of as related, were then separately administered under the jurisdiction of separate departments." p. 13.
- 1932 "Report on Provincial Policy on Administrative Methods in the matter of Direct Relief in Ontario" under William R. Campbell set standards for relief issuances which proved to be, "The notion of a standard policy and standard

rates...introducing some order and minimum justice into what had been a confusion of quarrels and complaints." pp. 17-18.
- the Unemployment Relief Act of 1935 when "Legally, anything could be done; practically, not much...municipal finances near collapse...defaulting on debentures." p. 20
- in the 1930s, David Croll, as a Minister in Ontario, held "three portfolios of Labour, Municipal Affairs and Public Welfare, and he administered unemployment relief as an interdepartmental concern." He held the three portfolios for purposes of co-ordination. p. 13.

Through it all and subsequent advances, carrying forward to the 1990s, all sorts of definitions of unemployment are and have been a background feature of income maintenance. (See Appendix XI review/report about NO FAULT OF THEIR OWN).

Clifford Williams, in Chapter 10, "Income Maintenance Developments," stated, "The federal government has continued to be an active, even eager participant in social-service development...The most relevant of...measures was the Canada Assistance Plan of 1966...But the term "Plan" was a misnomer: this was not a definite action plan to be carried out directly by the federal government." Dr. Williams could have also stated, as did I in Chapter 5 forward, "Its a good thing we have enduring Acts, Regulations and Policies as organizational phenomena come and go, came and went." (see "METAPHORS OF PUBLIC ADMINISTRATION", Chapter 4, forward)

APPENDIX XIV: STRAIGHT THROUGH THE HEART, by Maude Barlow & Bruce Campbell, Harper Collins Publishers Limited.[1]

I shouldn't be reminiscing and ruminating about 40 to 50 years ago when young social activists were using Carl Marx for their model in the 1950s and 1960s, yielding writings like STRAIGHT THROUGH THE HEART. This isn't to say that inspired rhetoric is confined to social activism of the 1990s. Neither is it to say that all social activists, some of whom quietly carry on in essential volunteer services, should be considered as part of echoing voice choruses.

I went looking for a book to review for the appendices of my study of THE CANADA ASSISTANCE PLAN, hoping to find a book similar to NO FAULT OF THEIR OWN, by James Struthers,[2] which I had reviewed in my book, THE WELFARE.[3] But STRAIGHT THROUGH THE HEART krept up on me, so to speak. Here it is in my abridged sort of review/report. I mentioned Carl Marx as the model of the 1950s and 1960s which captured attentions of the then radical, social activists, so I've used that sort of reflection in my criticism of the rhetoric of Barlow and Campbell. Northrop Frye's study of THE GREAT CODE reflected on the context of Marx much better than I can, so the following quote is offered here,

> "One of the earliest of third phase writers, Machiavelli, attempted
> to distinguish and isolate the tactical use of illusion in the art of
> ruling. For Rousseau civilization was largely an illusion

concealing a society of nature and reason; for Marx, the whole second-phase approach to language had become an ideology, or facade, of ascendent class authority; for Freud the language of consciousness was largely a screen concealing other motives for speech. To conservative thinkers, including Burke, the facade of authority in society revealed the real structure of that society."[4]

By the way, Northrop Frye's book, THE GREAT CODE indexed Karl Marx 4 times. And Frye indexed Marxism 8 times. Other historical thinkers approached such issues from other directions. Modern thinkers, such as Barlow and Campbell don't offer their writings amidst such an outline per se, but their approach implies contexts of written and spoken issues. It's up to their readers to follow up on such rhetorical manners. The CONTENTS of their book are as follows

The book isn't written precisely in chronolgical order, by time. For examples, here paraphrased from pages 12-25 of Chapter 1, reference to trade union membership for the years 1890, 1910, and 1920. Farmers' parties capturing 65 seats in the 1921 federal election. The Winnipeg General Strike of 1919. Mackenzie King committed to a welfare state in 1919, but he remained dedicated to a free market economy. In 1927 he passed old-age pension legislation. The financial crash of 1929 saw two competing ideologies meet head to head over opposing social policies. In Ontario, unemployment rose from 2 percent in 1929 to 36 percent in 1936. By 1936, one-third of Saskatchewan farmers were on relief. By 1937 two-thirds. By 1932, almost 100,000 homeless men were wandering the country, sleeping in alleys, riding the rails, growing restless in relief camps. Federal transfers to the provinces grew dramatically in social welfare from 2.5 percent in 1910 to

25.7 percent in mid-1930s. In 1936, Quebec forced all recipients into workfare. Mackenzie King governed Canada prior to and through the depression from 1921 to 1930 and from 1935 to 1948. R.B.Bennett had replaced King as Prime Minister from 1931 to 1935, but King returned and convinced that the worst was over thereafter reduced aid to the provinces by 25 percent in 1936 and by 34 percent in 1937. In 1933, an historic meeting of farmers, academics, social reformers, urban socialists, labour unions, and Social Gospel adherents founded the Co-operative Commonwealth Federation. Air Canada, CBC and the Bank of Canada were established in the 1930s. In 1938, King was forced by public opinion to spend money in the form of public works and housing to counteract a low in the business cycle. Canadians went to war in 1939. By 1943, only 0.3 percent of trade unionists were unemployed compared to 17 percent in 1939. The CCF grew to 20,000 in 1942, to 100,000 in 1944. Labour-union membership mushroomed to 700,000 by war's end. The CCF formed the government in Saskatchewan in 1944 and held power until 1962. In Ontario the CCF became the official opposition in 1943. In 1961, CCF became the New Democratic Party.

The 1940 Rowell-Sirois Report on Dominion-Provincial Relations established the principles of the modern Canadian state. 1943 reports on Social Security by Dr. Leonard Marsh; the Heagerty Report on Health Insurance; and the Curtis Report on Housing and Community Planning, and the 1944 White Paper on Employment and Income committed government to full employment. "These reports were not universally accepted. Powerful forces in business and the business Liberals in government were strongly opposed to full-scale implementation ...It would not be until the 1960s and 1970s that government investment in social welfare would again reach the level of the 1930s. In 1945, King introduced the first universal social program - family allowances for everyone with children under age seventeen." p. 22. Major political pressures and influences were from the left, Communism and socialism were on the rise; if capitalism was to survive real modifications would have to be made; thus King created the foundations for the welfare state. In the 1990s, business no longer feels the need to accomodate popular demands.

"Post-war Canada under the Liberals boomed. The gross national product doubled between 1950 and 1960. The St. Lawrence Seaway and the Trans Canada gas and oil pipelines were built." During the prosperous 1950s, the Liberals were largely able to rebuff calls for reform.........they did introduce the second major universal social program - old age security for those aged seventy and over - in 1952". p.24..."A limited form of Hospital insurance in 1957". p.25. and...a federal/provincial initiative the Unemployment Assistance Act. Unemployment grew in the later 1950s, and the Liberals were defeated in the 1957-58 election. The history is carried forward with a fervour about familiar images and events.

The authors of this book are decidedly negative about corporate power. Their persistent portrayals of corporate power attitudes vis-a-vis the community at large, distract readers who are looking for historical information. And some important history is missing. For example, there's nothing in the book about how provincial and federal governments had to financially aid bankrupt municipalities during the

Depression. Nor is there any record of Houses of Refuge which became chaotic refuges, in the midst of communities where local authorities had no knowledge about conditions existing in their communities, of crowded refuges with all sorts of distressed patients whom were undifferentiated in the treatments they received.

Economic analysis of the book, STRAIGHT THROUGH THE HEART is incomplete. To quote its reflection on significant federal government research, "Finance Department's own research of the growth of the debt since 1985 was due entirely to the compounding of interest on the original debt. Between 1985 and 1991, the government paid out a total of $200 billion in interest payments."... That statistic may be accurate, and it isn't my intention to blame the growth of government debt on social spending, but a reflection on a Statistics Canada study by Mimento and Cross must surely be incompletely reported by STRAIGHT THROUGH THE HEART. Any review of Social Security Statistics by Statistics Canada, from 1975 to 1991, contradicts the assertion, "The landmark Statistics Canada study by Mimento and Cross that government spending, and specifically social spending, held steady from 1975 to 1991." (See APPENDICES VIII, IX & X here above).

The economics of the debatable book by Barlow and Campbell can't be reviewed in detail here. They mainly oppose the global economy as though it's new, but controversial economics of world trade have been with the world for centuries, since before Canada became a nation. What is new is that world trade now seems to be working. Here's a pertinent quote from Paul A. Samuelson's text ECONOMICS, 1951, "Postwar International Cooperation. Economic isolation will not work. On this, if on no other proposition, (99%) of all economists are agreed. Nevertheless, economic isolation may again rear its head, because nations who ignore history are condemned to repeat it."[5]

Who is responsible for Canada's problems of industrial relations? There's probably as much, if not more history, between the lines of spoken and written history. This is true in the histories and practices of industrial relations, especially in conflicts between labour and managements. It can perhaps be as accurate to anticipate what might be included in histories 100 years hence as it is to speculate about what is missing about bygone years in histories today. Who is responsible for Canada's problems of industrial relations? Would the answer to such a question answer all questions about Canada's problems? Will history 100 years hence be able to state what was, or whom were, responsible for Canada's problems?

FOOTNOTES TO APPENDIX XIV: STRAIGHT THROUGH THE HEART

1. STRAIGHT THROUGH THE HEART by Maude Barlow & Bruce Campbell, Harper Collins Publishers Limited, Toronto, 1995, 259 pages, ISBN 0-00-255306-6.

2. NO FAULT OF THEIR OWN, by James Struthers, University of Toronto Press, 1983, 268 pages.

3. THE WELFARE, A Concise Archival History of Social Services, edited and published by Kenneth Coward, printed by Stan Brown Printers, Owen Sound 1994, 90 pages.

4. THE GREAT CODE, THE BIBLE AND LITERATURE, by Northrop Frye, published by the Penguin Group, Penguin Books of Canada Limited, 10 Alcorn Avenue, Toronto, Ontario,   Canada, M4V 3B2, ISBN 0-14-012928-6, 260 pages, p.16

5. ECONOMICS, by Paul A. Samuelson, published by McGraw Hill Book Company Inc., Toronto 1951, 762 pages, pp.682-683

APPENDICES XV, XVI, XVII
HISTORICAL MEMOIRS

APPENDIX XV: There are two parts to this appendix:

PART 1 NOTES FROM CORRESPONDENCE WITH G. C. McCLURE
PART 2 THE FEDERAL REGIONAL OFFICE OF CAP AT QUEEN'S PARK

PART 1. NOTES FROM CORRESPONDENCE WITH G. C. McCLURE, (retired 1985) former Federal Representative (Manager) of the Ontario Region; he administered the Canada Assistance Plan Agreement between the Federal Department of Health and Welfare and the Provincial Ministry of Community and Social Services.

The Canada Assistance Plan was cost shared through (HWC), the Department of Health and Welfare from 1966 to 1993. In 1993, the Department of Human Resources Development, Canada took over CAP. Before 1966, Categorical Programs of Disabled Persons's Allowances, Blind Person's Allowances and Old Age Allowances had been previously cost shared with the provinces; the federal government shared the expenditures which were incurred by the provinces for the programs at the rates of 75% for Blind Persons' Allowances and Disabled Persons' Allowances, and 50% for Old Age Allowances. Federal staffs were located in Provincial Capitals where they reviewed applications and they approved, for cost sharing, applicants who were shareable. The Categorical Programs would later become phased out when the Canada Assistance Plan came into effect.

Ontario enacted legislation of the Family Benefits Act, General Welfare Assistance Act, Child Welfare Act, Homes for Aged Act, and Childrens' Institutions Act, and other Acts for social services in Ontario. These legislations were based on "needs tests", unlike earlier legislations which had been by "means tests". The "needs tested" programs became funded under the Canada Assistance Plan Agreement, whereas the "means tested" programs had been funded under separate arrangements between the federal and provincial governments. "Needs tests" focus on the needs of individuals and families for basic needs, shelter and other needs, according to family sizes and ages of the children. Whereas "means tested" allowances were restricted payments of money, never to exceed certain stipulated amounts.

The Unemployment Assistance Act of 1956 covered Public Welfare and Homes for the Aged. Eligibility was based on a "means test" for applicants who made applications in municipalities. G. C. McClure administered the federal office in Ontario under the Unemployment Assistance Act from 1964 onward; and he became Federal Representative, Ontario when the Canada Assistance Plan was legislated. The federal Audit Services Bureau came into the scene of the Ontario office after CAP was under way. (See NOTES OF CONVERSATIONS AND CORRESPONDENCE WITH RALPH CHAYTOR in Appendix XVII). Headquarters for the Unemployment Assistance Act (1956) was based in Ottawa, headed by the

Director, Dr. Splane, and by the Assistant Director, R. Draper. Des Byrne was a Charterted Accountant in Ottawa for the Unemployment Assistance Act organization. They continued in Headquarters when the Canada Assistance Plan Division was created. CAP was made retroactive to April 1, 1965. Dr. Splane was later promoted to Director General and subsequently became an Assistant Deputy Minister of Health and Welfare.

The Prime Minister of Canada with Dr. Splane, and with Dr. Willard, the Deputy Minister of Health and Welfare Canada, created the long term view of the Canada Assistance Plan. It was anticipated the mandate of the Division would grow for the benefit of "persons in need".

Expenditures of programs, under provincial legislation, (were) shared with the federal government under Agreements with the provinces according to the Canada Assistance Plan. Under the Agreements, pertinent, provincial legislation (were) approved by the Canada Assistance Plan and listed in Schedule "C" of the Agreements. Other listings of Homes of Special Care in Shedules "A" and Welfare Services in Schedule "B" (were) also required for cost sharing, according to the Agreements.

Administration costs of the province and the municipalities, such as salaries and benefits, were included in the Canada Assistance Plan Agreements, between Canada and the provinces, including Ontario, from a Base Year. Expenditures incurred by the province, for administration of shareable programs, (were) shared with the Base Year amount deducted each year.

Norman Cragg entered the picture later when Dr. Splane left the Division of the Canada Assistance Plan. Norman Cragg became Director General and subsequently became an Assistant Deputy Minister. Later still, after he had built up the headquaters' staff for CAP, he went to British Columbia.

R. Draper went to a job on the Health side of Health and Welfare, Canada.

Des Byrne, while employed at the Canada Assistance Plan Division, became promoted to Director General, and he later became an Assistant Deputy Minister of Health and Welfare. He's a graduate, professional accountant, regarded by G. C. McClure to be one of the best who always gave direct answers to McClure's questions.

The provincial department in Ontario was originally the Public Welfare Department, which became Social Services, and later became the Ministry of Community and Social Services of Ontario.

Earlier heads of the Ontario organization included
        Dr. Cliff Williams,
        William (Bill) L. Smith,
        Dr. James Band
        Mr. M. Borzak

Here follows a speech given by G. C. McClure on an occasion at Queen's Park when the 25th Aniversary of CAP was celebrated - 23 September 1992

Ladies and Gentlemen:

It is most appropriate, I feel, that we should take time to remember the far reaching effects that the Canada Assistance Act and Regulations has had in the field of Social Service, for Canada in general and Ontario in particular.

It is also right and just that we should pause for a little while to recall those sincerely dedicated and far-sighted federal, and provincial officials, who participated directly and indirectly in the creation of the C.A.P. Act --- for they have left a lasting impression in the field of Social Service which, to my mind, is second to none in this wonderful Canada of ours.

The Ottawa officials, led at that time, by the far-sighted Dr. Willard, Deputy Minister of Health and Welfare, Canada: coupled with the able assistance of his senior officials in the persons of Dr. Dick Splane, Messrs Ron Draper, Des Byrne, Norm Cragg, and many others. These officials realized that a new concept of the federal legislation was needed to cover Child Care, The Aged, The Disabled, The Blind, and persons in Distress Circumstances.

By utilizing the experience gained in administering "The Unemployment Assistance Act of 1956", they developed a completely new, and to some, a radical approach based on the "needs" of the individual, coupled with shared costs for providing these services. Before this new and far reaching concept could be implemented, it was essential that communication with, and contributions by, provincial officials be established. In this way they would not only be made aware of the over-all concept, but would have the opportunity to contribute to the proposed legislation while it was still in the development stage.

In Ontario, we were fortunate at that time, to have individuals who were extremely gifted, and had the ability to foresee the future "needs" in the Social Service fields of this province.

The contributions made by such outstanding persons as Dr. James S. Band, Deputy Minister of Community and Social Services; Mr. Marm Borzak, Dr. Dorothea Crittenden, Mr. Doug Rutherford, Mr. John G. Anderson, Mr. Jack McKnight, Mr. Earl Ludlow, and many others, contributed greatly to the success of this new concept which became known as the Canada Assistance Act and Regulations.

Indeed, the success of the C.A.P. is indicated in the fact that it has been in operation for MORE-THAN-A-QUARTER-OF-A-CENTURY.

Those of us who were present in the early years can be justly proud of the contributions made by the C.A.P. Act (and the 27 Provincial Listed Legislations) for it established new and broader concepts in the field of Social Services which are still evident to this day.

But what about the future in this ever changing and challenging field of Social Services in the 90s?

I feel certain that the present administrators, at the federal, provincial and municipal levels, will be equally successful in finding ways of meeting the growing demand for Social Services, in spite of the slow growth of the present economy. Certainly, we of those early years, wish you every success in your future endeavours.

Mr. Toastmaster, ladies and gentlemen, it has been a pleasure to be with you at this very special occasion, and I thank you most sincerely for your time, your courtesy, and your attention.

PART 2. THE FEDERAL REGIONAL OFFICE OF CAP AT QUEEN'S PARK

Our boss, Mr. G. C. McClure, as the Federal Representative for CAPs Regional Office in Ontario, directed how we should review the records of cost details in Ontario's provincial expenditures with regard to eligibility and shareability for social services, to review the costs which Canada would or would not share with Ontario. (see Appendix V, PART 1, above NOTES from G. C. McClure about the early organization of the Canada Assistance Plan). "If it isn't in the Acts and Regs of the province, and if it isn't in the Schedules and Agreement, of the Canada Assistance Plan, it isn't shareable by Canada." Viola Bowen would instruct new staff members at the Regional, CAP office in Ontario. She had been working in the Regional Office with the indirect functions of CAP since 1968, and she trained me on the job. I was also trained by other staff members - Paul Kutty, Gwen Head and Dave Cordick. Irene Sanderson came on staff soon after I joined the office in 1979. We were a crew, and we all trained new staff members who joined the Regional Office of CAP in Ontario, including Derek Johnston and Isabel Belanger. We had all held other positions in the public service of the Government of Canada before we worked with the Canada Assistance Plan.

Viola Bowen retired in 1984 after (30) thirty years of service with Health and Welfare, Canada. Paul Kutty left our office in 1988 when he became an advisor in the Ministry of Community and Social Services. Viola and Paul and I had often worked together on review projects, at our office, and at field offices. During breaks from the details of the reviews, we rarely discussed politics, in keeping with the non-partisanship of public service. Although we each had our own political opinions, we couldn't allow conflicts of interests of our opinions to distract the regional office where we were involved with legislations and policies affecting social services, and cost sharing arrangements between the federal and provincial governments. Functions of political decision making determined such legislations, arrangements and policies. The Canada Assistance Plan Agreement, between the governments of the Province of Ontario and Canada, was co-signed by federal and provincial ministers in 1966 when the Act was legislated. Whereby cost sharing between the federal and provincial governments, for approved social services, complied with terms of the Agreement of the Canada Assistance Plan. And social services' legislations of the province were approved, or disapproved for cost sharing, in compliance with terms of the Agreement.

When I visited with Viola in 1991, as I was preparing to retire, our conversation, about many past years of public services, found its way to specific Acts and Regulations of social services, and Viola spontaneously recited the dates of legislations she had memorized many years ago, going back to categorical, social services' legislations of 1952, including Blind Persons' Allowances, Disabled Persons' Allowances and Old Age Assistance. In 1967, Viola and Elaine McDowell, working from Ottawa Headquarters, travelled across Canada to Provincial offices with regard to phasing out the Categorical Agreements, with the advent of the Canada Assistance Plan Act and the CAP Agreements of 1966. (See Appendix XIII report/review about DECADES OF SERVICE for an outline of categorical and other programs which preceded the Canada Assistance Plan Act).

The Federal Regional Office of CAP moved out of Queen's Park accomodation in 1990 to an office on Bay Street south of Queen Street in Toronto. This Regional Office for Ontario moved to 25 St. Clair Ave. East, 4th Floor in 1993 when the Canada Assistance Plan was assigned to the Department of Human Resources Development, Canada; and the Department of Health and Welfare (HWC) reverted back to the Department of Health.

APPENDIX XVI

CONVERSATIONS AND CORRESPONDENCE WITH GEORGE ROMANSON, former Administrator with the Department of Community Services, Metropolitan Toronto. (retired 1990)

George Romanson started his career in social services as a Welfare Visitor for the City of Toronto where he was employed for two years from 1958 to 1960.

1960 to 1964, he was employed by the Province of Ontario in the administrative offices of General Welfare. At his provincial job, he was responsible for liaison with municipalities, and with other provinces, about allowances granted by Ontario municipalities to "persons-in-need" who had recently moved to Ontario from other provinces. The contacts with other provinces were necessary in order to ascertain whether or not recent welfare recipients, from other provinces, were in receipt of welfare from the other provinces. And, the recipients of welfare in Ontario, with residency of less than a year in Ontario, are classified as "non-residents". George Romanson checked information about residency, on behalf of the Province of Ontario, because the province reimburses municipalities 100% of welfare payments to "non-resident" cases, and residency information about the recipients had to be verified. Information about non-residents, coming to Ontario from the Province of Quebec, had to be obtained through the Quebec's Church Diocese offices when welfare was administered under the Catholic Church in Quebec in the early 1960s.

OTHER RANDOM COMMENTS

Municipalities in Ontario also used the term "non-resident" within each municipality to describe each recipient who had moved into their municipality from another Ontario municipality. Expenditures by each municipality, on behalf of these "non-residents", who moved into a municipality from other Ontario municipalities, were "charge-backs" to the municipalities from where they came. When George Romanson was Commissioner of Welfare for the Borough of East York, his department had to count the recipients of East York, who came from other municipalities, and whom he "charged-back" to the other municipalities. And East York reimbursed other municipalities for allowances issued to welfare recipients in the other municipalities, for "non-residents" from East York who had moved to other municipalities.

George Romanson was Commissioner of Welfare at the Borough of East York in 1964, and he later went to Metro Welfare as Administrator of the North York Office in 1968. He was subsequently transferred, as Administrator, to other offices of Metro Social Services.

Ryerson Institute started to provide courses in 1966, granting their first certificates in 1968. Ryerson later granted Degrees for Social Service graduates. OMSSA, the Ontario Municipal Social Services Association, had some part in lobbying Ryerson to provide the courses.

George Romanson and John Anderson helped to establish the Ontario Municipal Social Service Association (OMSSA). Don McKenzie, Ray Tomlinson and John Sylvester, of Metropolitan Toronto's (Welfare) Social Services Department, were also active in the early years of OMSSA.

Metro's Department of Welfare became Metro Social Services on 5 May 1970. (later Metro Community Services) The department, mainly concerned with administration of General Welfare Assistance, also provides Child Welfare subsidies to CAS's, services of Homes for the Aged, Subsidized Housing, Day Care, Nursing and Homemaker Services, and Hostels. The Men's Hostel, Seaton House was on Seaton Street from 1931 until the building on George Street was built in 1958.

Day Care had its start in the years of wartime when working mothers, who were employed in war plants, placed their children in day care centres. Many of the centres were revitalized by the Department of Welfare.

The following names were randomly recalled by George Romanson, in conversations about significant developments in the early years - 1967 onward - of Metropolitan Toronto's Welfare Department. Many other persons were employed in the department, and those who are still in the department's Social Services Division, which has been changed several times through the years. Names and functions of past and present personnel can be obtained through the CLIENT SERVICE AND INFORMATION UNIT, 12th Floor, Metro Hall, 55 John Street, Station 1123, Toronto, Ontario M5V 3C6.

Most of the following persons were responsible for functions providing direct social services. They had direct contacts with clients.

Anderson, John came from the provincial welfare office in Chatham to Queen's Park to replace the deceased Arthur Bosanquet, head of General Welfare Administration. In 1967, Anderson went to Metro Toronto as Commissioner of the new Welfare Department. He later returned to Queen's Park as an ADM.

Ashbury, Sid - Provincial Relief - involved with Work Camps in the 1930s and later with Indian Welfare.

Band, James - early Deputy Minister of Ontario's Department of Social Services.

Boyce, Wilf - Metro Head Office Social Worker in the 1967 organization of the Metro Welfare Department.

Campbell, Joe worked with the Province of Ontario, involved with formations of Welfare Offices in Ontario's Regional Municipalities.

Croll, David - early Minister of Ontario's Department of Welfare.

Cully, Tom - Head Office Social Worker in the 1967 Metro Welfare Department. He had been with City of Toronto Welfare, and his education at the School of Social Work was sponsored for a year by the City. His second year was sponsored by Metro.

Fleming, John had been with the Province of Ontario, involved with formations of Welfare Offices of Regional Municipalities. He transferred to the municipal level, and in the early 1970's he went to Metro Social Services. He was the first Deputy Commissioner of Social Services at Metro.

Goldenberg, Carl - Goldenberg Commission recommended amalgamation of the services into Metropolitan Toronto. General Welfare Assistance wasn't part of the Department until 1967; the Municipality of Metropolitan Toronto had been formed in 1953.

McKenzie, Don - first Chief District Administrator of Metro Welfare Department, 1968. He had been Commissioner of Welfare at North York, and before that he had been with the Province of Ontario.

McMillan, Gord was a clerk with the City of Toronto Department of Welfare at West Toronto when George Romanson started as a Welfare Visitor at the same office. McMillan later became a General Welfare Administrator.

Morris, Robina - City of Toronto Commissioner of Welfare went to General Welfare Administration for the Province of Ontario when Metro Welfare was formed.

Ralph, Ed was employed in the Province of Ontario's office of General Welfare

Administration when George Romanson was working at the same office.

Richardson, Doug - Administrator at the George Street Office at the start of GWA in the Department in 1967. He had been with the Department of Welfare with the City of Toronto.

Rupert, Howard - 1958 City of Toronto's Commissioner of Welfare, before Robina Morris.

Smith, Charlie - Commissioner of Welfare for the Borough of Scarborough before General Welfare Assistance became part of the Metro Department. Patti LeBar was a clerk in the Scarborough Welfare Department at that time.

Smith, Gord - Administrator at East Toronto office of Metro Welfare 1960s, he later became a second, Chief District Administrator when Metro was shared between him and Don McKenzie.

Smith, R. J. was an Interim Commissioner of Welfare for Metropolitan Toronto for Homes for the Aged and Housing, before General Welfare Assistance became part of the department and was administered separately by the separate townships, (which became Boroughs of Metro) all of which, except the Borough of East York, became cities within Metro.

Sylvester, John was Commissioner of Welfare of York Township; he became Welfare Administrator at York Borough, of Metro Social Services. He also served awhile as Chief District Administrator of Metro Social Services when Don McKenzie took ill.

Tomlinson, Ray - Commissioner of Welfare for the Township of Etobicoke since the 1950s; he became a Director at Metro Welfare in the 1960s, eventually to become Commissioner of Welfare of Metropolitan Toronto in the 1970s.

Turnbull, Bill - Head Office Social Worker in 1967 Metro Welfare Department.

Vernon, Joe - Commissioner of Welfare at East York to 1964.

Warriner, Walter - Head Office Social Worker in 1967 Metro Welfare Department.

For a more comprehensive and particularized history of Municipal Social Services in Ontario, see DECADES OF SERVICE by Clifford J. Williams. A review/report of DECADES OF SERVICE is included in the appendices here.

APPENDIX XVII

NOTES FROM CONVERSATIONS AND CORRESPONDENCE WITH RALPH
CHAYTOR, former Auditor with Audit Services Bureau of the Department of Supply
and Services. (Retired December 1989).

The Federal Audit Service Bureau was first formed in 1942, and the Department of
Supply and Services took over the unit in 1968. The Bureau was renamed as the
Audit Services Group in 1990.

According to Ralph Chaytor, assignments of Audit Services Bureau, changed
through the years. ASB auditors, as part of the Finance Department, were assigned
to do audits at agencies and firms wherever the federal government had spent
money. But in later years, ASB was only assigned to do audits where the government
had long term agreements or contracts.

Methods of doing audits by ASB also changed. In 1980-1981, Ralph supervised
ASB audits of projects of (LIP) - Local Initiative Projects where audits found that
many of the projects were not spending monies according to publicly stated
purposes, but the ASB contracts, to audit the Local Initiative Projects, were only to
ensure that allocated money was spent. Allocation Audits of (LIP) projects
disregarded inappropriate spending of government funding.

ASB was only required to verify that funding allocations had been spent, and that
further funding allocations were needed to enable the projects to continue. In this
sort of audit, compliance rules for spending money, according to publicly stated
purposes, were not required. Compliance Audits verify that public funds have
been spent effectively, because they require specified expenditures to be spent in
compliance with publicly stated purposes. Furthermore, compliance audits verify
that the specified expenditures were spent according to contracted rules and
agreements.

Value-for-money audits are also different than Compliance Audits. Ralph concurred
with the following quotation, from an IPAC article by Professor D. G. Hartle,

"The beginning of wisdom would be to abandon the overly simplistic concept of
value-for-money auditing and accept the fact that assessing cost effectiveness of
government programs...is an extremely complex matter that entails not only the
assessment of the extent to which governments are doing "the right thing right" but
also whether they are doing the the right thing right for the benefit of the right
people using inputs from the right sources. Let us stop pretending that these
questions are "answerable" in strictly professional terms by accountants,
management consultants and economists". This quote is in conclusion of Professor
Hartle's article about "Perceptions of the Expenditure Budget Process" in which
he argues for "in-depth assessment of evaluation efforts of government with respect
to the three Es of economy, efficiency and effectiveness".[1] (See also APPENDIX
XIX, FOOTNOTE 2).

Audit Services Bureau, of the Department of Supply and Services, under yearly contracts, with the Department of Health and Welfare, from 1967 to 1989, audited the financial arrangements of the Canada Assistance Plan Agreement in Ontario, between Health and Welfare Canada and the Ministry of Community and Social Services of Ontario. The Canada Assistance Plan was administered by the Department of Health and Welfare from 1966 until 1993. In 1993, the Department of Human Resources Development, Canada took over CAP.

Audit Services Bureau, in the Ontario Regional Office of CAP, was mainly concerned with final claims which were submitted to CAP's Federal Representative of HWC by the Ministry of Community and Social Services of Ontario (MCSS). ASB auditors also accompanied Federal Field Officers on field trips to do audits of specific agencies, which were selected for audit samples, or to audit particular problems which had been noted in final claims.

Different sorts of final claims were submitted by MCSS on CAP. Some of the final claims were for specific programs such as claims for Ontario Childrens' Aid Societies (CASs) - all 52 CASs (as of 1990) in the Province of Ontario submitted their year-end reports to MCSS, and MCSS extracted non-shareable costs from Cost Detail Expenditure Reports of the CASs, and submitted a total claim on CAP each year.

In the Regional CAP office, cost details, of expenditures of each CAS, were reviewed by CAP Field Officers to be sure the non-shareable costs had been extracted and to verify compliance with cost-sharing criteria of Canada Assistance Plan Agreement. Year-end final claims were then passed on to ASB for the audit, according to Audit Terms of Reference which had been agreed to between ASB and CAP.

Most other programs of the Ministry of Community and Social Services didn't require as much detailed review as did the expenditure reports about Childrens Aid Societies, except for programs under separate Agreements of Indian Welfare, and of Vocational Rehabilitation Services. Details of expenditures for most programs claimed on CAP, which had been reviewed through each year by CAP officers in the Ontario Region, and observations arising from such reviews, were sufficient for year end final claims purposes.

Other sorts of final claims include all programs which were claimed by MCSS on CAP in Final, Final Claims which were claimed each year. The Ontario Region of CAP usually picked up all the unsettled observations which had been made through the year, or carried forward from prior years, and included the information as unsettled in the file of the Final Final Claims. The reviews of the FF Claims by CAP Field Officers were followed up by ASB audits. Audit Reports by Audit Services Bureau were attached to the files of Final, Final Claims which were used for settlements between Ontario and Canada.

Financial documents, including claims, signed with an "Auditor's Comment" are unacceptable in Final Final Claims. The ASB auditors in our regional office took exception to Ontario's practice of signing off Final Final Claims with an "Auditor's

Comment". The auditors of ASB contended that the provincial auditor should certify Final, Final Claims as accurate before the claims are submitted to Canada, and Mel Berger, Ralph Chaytor's supervisor with ASB, took up the issue with CAP's, Federal Representative, G. C. McClure. Eventually, the issue led to changes in the way Final, Final Claims were handled by the Province of Ontario.

RALPH CHAYTOR

Ralph was employed with Audit Services Bureau for 22 years. When he started to work for ASB in 1967, Audit Services Bureau was under the Department of Finance, where auditors were classified as Treasury Auditors. As an auditor for Audit Services Bureau of the Department of Supply and Services, he started at the Canada Assistance Plan (CAP), Regional Ontario Office, in 1983.

FOOTNOTE TO APPENDIX XVII

1. CANADIAN PUBLIC ADMINISTRATION (Journal) "Perceptions of the expenditure budget process" by Douglas G. Hartle p. 448, Volume 32, #3, Fall 1989, pp. 427-448.

APPENDICES XVIII, XIX REPORTS

APPENDIX XVIII CANADIAN PERIODICALS

Here's a random sampling from CANADIAN PERIODICAL INDEX, for examples since 1920, which indicate many variables by decades, (some of the indexes include a full decade) beginning 1920-1937 to 1948-1959, then sampling each year from 1960 to 1969, then using only mid decade of 1975, 1985 & 1995[1] for the samples, asking, How many pages of poems are in the index in selected years? How many titles of the poems include the first person "I" and possessive "My"? How many include the second person "You", and its possessive, "Your"?

YEAR	PAGES of POEMS	"I"	"My"	"You"	"Your"
1920-37 all years	pp.424-439	15	8	3	1
1938-47 all years	pp.1520-1590 large pages	29	24	8	0
1948-59 all years	pp.875-897 large pages	33	27	7	1
(smaller journals, hereonward)*					
1960	pp. 215-221	2	6	0	0
1961	pp. 270-278 (1/2 of p.270)	4	2	0	0
1962	pp. 282-288	5	4	0	1
1963	pp. 318-325 (1/2 of p.318)	6	6	1	0
1964	pp. 357-364	8	2	1	1
1965	pp. 349-356	4	4	1 "You & I"	2
1966	pp. 370-378 (1/2 of p.370)	11	6	0	0
1967	pp. 354-362	10	7	1	3
1968	pp. 330-336 (1/2 of p.330)	5	7	0	2
1969	pp. 369-374 (1/2 of p.374)	6	3	2	1
1975	pp. 363-369 (1/2 of p.363)	3	4	1	2
1985**	pp. 503-506	5	1	2	0
1986-1993***1995****	pp. 1071-1081 (1/2 of p.1071)	10	10	5 +1"You're"	1

* Before 1960, the journals were huge
** Up to 1985, published by Canadian Library Association
*** 1986-1993, published by INFO GLOBE
**** 1994 onward, published by GALE Canada, a division of THOMPSON Canada Limited.

Canadian periodicals are indexed extensively in available reference volumes of libraries. Available for research, for example, in volumes of the publication of CANADIAN INDEX TO PERIODICALS, (1948 to 1963 published as CANADIAN INDEX TO PERIODICALS AND DOCUMENTARY FILMS). A student of literature might use the index for a thesis on poems and poetry to create data for a history about Canadian literature. Or, another student might use lists of poetry in the INDEX to search for symbolic significance in usages of some words. For examples, seeking underlying, unconscious or esoteric, symbolic meanings in written or spoken words such as "I", "My", "You" or "Your".

Likely, other titles of more poems starting with "I", "My", "You" and "Your" were published during the selected years, but the CANADIAN INDEX OF PERIODICALS is a substantial sampling source; (from 1948 to 1963, it was published as CANADIAN INDEX OF PERIODICALS AND DOCUMENTARY FILMS); many logistical and other changes have happened to the "INDEX" over the years in its publishing history, including changes of the printer, the editors and the publisher. Another source of information, CANADIAN POETRY, isn't referenced in my research; it's a journal devoted to the study of poetry from all periods in Canada, published twice yearly.[2]

Editors:

1920-1937	Grace Heggie and 4 others.
1938-1946	May L. Newton
1947	Dorothy Davidson
1948-1959	Isabel Bradley and 2 others
1960	Margaret Wodehouse
1961	Lenore Aedy
1962-1972	Margaret Wodehouse
1975	Sylvia Morrison
1985	Edith Auckland
1995	Kathryn O'Handley

My above sampling, and comments about sources of samples, isn't intended to suggest that organization charts of publishers of the "INDEX" over the years would be especially significant to lead to the contents of what was published. It simply seems to me, students will miss many publishing and publisher changes and stabilities through years and decades, and consequently mishandle significance of indexed poems and poetry if they don't look into histories of indexes of periodicals. For example, the above sampling shows weighted word usages through years and decades.

The contents of Chapter 5, "CANADIAN MEDIA", is somewhat introductory to this APPENDIX XVIII. Canadian Periodical Index consented to use of quotes from editions 1920-1937, 1938-1947, 1948-1959, Volumes 13, 14, 15, 16, onward to 1969 Volumes 28. 38, 48.

And, the sampling I used for the above data from the INDEXES of selected years, is different than the data available from the STANDARD RATE AND DATA SERVICE (SRDS), which publishes data from their monthly ad rates directory, with information about production specifications, and with information about circulations of hundreds of magazine titles and other data information, published in the U.S.A. where population is ten times that of Canada. It's an "Audit Bureau of Circulations" about American periodicals - Canadian magazines such as Maclean's aren't included. SRDS does record information about TIME magazine; presumably SRDS records distinguish between TIME in the U.S.A. and TIME outside the U.S.A.. And a book titled THE MAGAZINE 2nd edition, by Leonard Mogel, A Folio: Book, published in Chester Connecticut, 1988, is a good source of information, regarding organization charts about magazine publishers, insofar as that sort of information would be pertinent as a lead to the contents of what was published.

Might there be any sort of negative effects from extensive awareness about marketing periodicals? Not the kinds of negative effects implied or accused about pornography, nor effects novelists work among on written and typed pages and in multi media in many, many languages - some languages unknown to mankind, some spoken or screamed, some mute, also archtypically in dreams, as though in whirlpools and undercurrents. The negative effects which could occur might develop from too much sensitivity by periodicals to market forces, at the expense of distractions from keener reasoning about whatever are the reasons d'etre of periodicals. These comments, by the way, aren't intended as warnings, as though community conflicts lurk in strategies of product marketing. Problems of published reasoning were in the culture of publishing long before product marketing techniques were developed.

In the history with which we're concerned here, we don't need to go back so far as the earliest culture of publishing to learn about manners of reasoning. Early journalism, for our puposes, is recorded in archival, periodical articles which reveal historical details to researchers. Students who want journalism experience in the study of social services, of early and middle twentieth century decades, can study periodical indexes noted in FOOTNOTES 3. 4. & 5. And actual preserved articles, and microfilmed articles, are also available, there to discover particular themes of each decade which weren't each all one thing or another. Other themes also emerged, some related to the major themes, but different. Years and decades from now, students using indexes will find information digitally recorded, and available in many varieties of data processing peripherals.

This study about THE CANADA ASSISTANCE PLAN can't wander any further astray into all sorts of thematic differences, interesting as they may be, in realizing all sorts of inspirations were at play. Could satirical questions inspire a focus on reason. How should social services be measured? If by volume, weights or quantities? If by time, when? If by distance, where? If by whom, whom? If not at all, why not? If replies could answer the questions, wouldn't they be widely influenced by divergent and hopelessly entangled agreements and disagreements. The dominant answer emerging from the entanglemts, of course, isn't of satire but of expenditure.

A 1966 speech quoted in the PREFACE was made to the Ontario Welfare Council by a senior, federal administrator, Norman Cragg in the beginning of the Canada Assistance Plan. The following quote is from his speech, "The Canada Welfare Council, in 1957, was able to draw upon the resources of many councils across Canada and other voluntary groups as well as public bodies in preparing its well-known and influential policy statement on "Social Security for Canada". In his statement on the Canada Assistance Plan made in the House on April 6th, 1965, the Prime Minister referred particularly to the wide support for a comprehensive program of public assistance that had been expressed by welfare organizations and authorities including the Canada Welfare Council." It can reasonably be assumed, Maclean's magazine was interested in such public initiatives, even though Maclean's didn't really become a news magazine, until 1978.

MACLEAN'S MAGAZINE

News features are, and news in general is, constantly changing in Canadian magazines; Maclean's, Canada's Weekly Newsmagazine is now advertized as publishing, "What Matters To Canadians"; Many of the following notes are about contents of Maclean's with regard to articles and items of news. This study about social services doesn't quote from Maclean's articles and items, so the format is more like an index than reviews of articles and items of news. Complete articles are available on COMPUSERVE "Maclean's On Line" see inside Maclean's for their phone number. Also, a librarian told me that distributors of all magazines provide computer files on discs about articles contained in each of the magazines. Articles and copies of Maclean's are kept as historical microfilmed copies in libraries. Some original archival copies of Maclean's, available in some libraries, are rather tattered but interesting all the same.

Although governments weren't and aren't the only players among social organizations, this history of THE CANADA ASSISTANCE PLAN is mainly about government programs. Since government programs are dependent on public financing, and government intervention affect economics, financial news and information is a large part of the study, (see APPENDICES VIII to X). Following selections from Maclean's aren't intended to advertise the magazine nor any of its columns and contributors. News articles and items probably get published in Maclean's when space is available for particular types of articles and items, and also according to several other variables of publishing a news magazine in Canada.

As noted in FOOTNOTES as follow, regarding APPENDIX XVIII, Maclean's Magazine Index, 1914-1937 is available at or from the Public Library, London, Ontario[6]. A variety of news subjects are indexed for 1914-1937, and as might be expected there are subjects, not necessarily related to each other, but in effect particularly historical by decades. News trends of the decades were mainly about the following subjects,

1910s Social changes and World War I.
1920s Stabilized economics were reflected in the news. (although unemployment was up and down through the decade. - see DECADES OF SERVICE p.15). [7]
1930s The Great Depression was featured in articles (but not as often as might be expected).

Later indexes cover the 1940s, 50s, 60s, 70s and 1980s.
1940s Featured news about World War II.
1950s Korean War news (in the early 50s) amidst all sorts of news through the decade.

Readings from actual, archival magazine articles of 1938 will find news proposals about "Unemployment Insurance" and "National Health Insurance." Wartimes articles were featured in copies of Maclean's from the 1940s.

In early issues of Maclean's, Col. J.B. Maclean appeared in articles or items of news of Maclean's magazine, sometimes in photos accompanied by personage(s), such as Ontario's Lieutenant Governor. The present owner, Ted Rogers, wouldn't likely appear in articles or items of news of Maclean's, accompanied by high ranking, influential political persons, such as Ontario's Premier nor with Ontario's Lieutenant Governor. Over the years, MACLEAN'S, like other news sources, published and continues to publish "Letters to the Editor" Address "Maclean's Magazine Letters, 777 Bay Street Toronto, Ont, M5W 1A7;" "The Mail" can also be accessed by E-mail and by Fax, as indicated on "The Mail" page of Maclean's. "Letters to the Editor" of all sorts of news' publications, including newspapers and periodicals, express opinions in many ways. Sometimes, Maclean's reveals data about volumes of "mail" received on topics which have been published in the magazine. The space affects and is affected by the times.

MACLEAN'S SHORT NEWS ITEMS

All sorts of cross-referencing, which would be necessary in an elaborate research project, hasn't been attempted here. To begin, from research of "News Items", the sampling is of 1995&96, 1997, 1998 and 1999 in mainly financial news, affecting governments and government services. All sorts of news isn't attended here. But some news affecting government expenditure will have exceptional affects on government budgets. Attempts are made to capture these. All sectors of Canadian affairs weren't regularly captioned in MACLEAN'S news items, except health news which is regularly reported; lately, other new captions carry readers to and through questions of, and/or, who, how, where, when, what.

Here follows information gleaned from reviewing financial items and other pertinent news; MACLEAN'S financial statistics are mainly from "Statistics Canada", but other information sources are used too. 1995&1996 samplings were preliminary, and samplings of subsequent years, were more rigorous; all the samples, although hastily composed are intuitively significant. "Intuition" in this context isn't to imply the following headings are mechanical signals.

Research data re "Maclean's Short News Items" are on the next page, 157.

SHORT ITEMS of NEWS	1995&96	1997	1998	1999
Budget	11	3		
Unemployment & Jobs & Employment	11	10	11	10
Economy	9	27	3	5
Tax			3	
Welfare	3			
Dollar		4		4
Interest Rates & Inflation (up & down)		2	8	11
Stock Market		3		
Pay		2		
Mergers & Investments			3	
Bankruptcies			3	
Internet				4
Labour				3

Other Items 1995&96:
2 each -   Health, Tax;
1 each -   audit, CPP, child poverty, dollar value, child support, families, fedralsm, inflation, protests, seniors, universities, youth, home resales, retail sales, international news.
Other Items 1997:
2 each -   child abuse, bankruptcies, interest rates:
1 each -   youth detention, advocate, CPP, CAS, charity, education, help wanted
Other Items 1998:
2 each -   housing, real estate, auto sales, rawmatrl prices, strkes, mortges
1 each -   Aids, Alta budgt, homeless, trde, industry, CPP, inhertnce, US visits Can., persnal debt, efficncy, trvl, smmr slmp, success, pverty, market, pay, dollar, travel, inheritance, foreign reserves.
Other Items 1999:
2 each -   government debt, oil&gas prices
1 each -   farm news, tourism, immigration, unemployment, tax, business activity, stock market, housing prices, mortgages, RRSP, household debts, boat people, retirees, young offenders, day care, GDP, stocks

MACLEAN'S MAJOR NEWS ARTICLES

The following comparative samplings data were assembled out of "news" articles when I researched into MACLEAN'S beyond the slogan, "What matters to Canadians". I've omitted many sorts of "news", and selected topics or themes handling concerns and issues which affect Canada's Social Services and Social Security. Sometimes, a topic or theme, featured in an edition of MACLEAN'S, is in several articles, and the separate articles are usually contributed by several different editors or by several different contributors. For example, - "Homelessness", and other topics or themes, appeared in several articles of 1 edition; in the example of "Homelessness", my sampling of the edition counted all articles about the topic, "Homelessness" as 1 theme only. But of course, as the topic or theme appeared again in other editions, it was counted the same way again in each edition. For example, "Election'97" was featured in several editions through 1997 and was counted the same way again etc. Many articles on topics or themes aren't topical here, although the articles may be incidental to issues and concerns of the topics and themes I've researched. International news, on every sort of topic isn't included here. And most public market issues and concerns, neither upward nor downward, they're not attended here. (See Chapter 5, "CANADIAN MEDIA")

MAJOR NEWS ARTICLES	1995&96	1997	1998	1999
Budget	11	8	5	3
Economy & Inflation	5			
Welfare	3			
Election'97		5		
Manitoba Flood		3		
Ice Storm			3	
Candn Dollr down			4	
Homelessness			4	
Volitility			4	
Jobs			4	
Business, Mergers, Lobbying			9	4
Labour				5
Internet				7
Boat people				3
Inuit			5	
Farmers				3
Taxes				3
Education				5
Aboriginal Culture				3

1995&96 Other Articles:
2 of each -   education, G.S.T.
1 of each -   taxes, B.C. vote, C.P.P, co-production breakdown, mining, protest, a poll.
1997 Other Articles:
2 of each -   advocacy, charity, health, polls
1 of each -   child poverty, C.P.P. fiscal facts, interest rates,investments, Ontario urban living.
1998 Other Articles:
2 each -   global economy.
1 each -   tax, intrest rts, retail, phone rates, farm income, unions.
1999 Other Articles: [8]
2 each -   tragedies, business forecasts, social union, elections
1 each -   periodicals, depression, manners, autos, street people, productivity, Rights, money, fedrl/provncl, seniors abuse, help wanted, homeless, law, politics, economy.

CONCLUSION from the sampling: the above data, of approximately four years review, has greater conclusive significance for data analysts, perhaps more from what's missing than from what's there. One noticeably missing element is inflation. Standard news industry questions and answers are reflected by sampling and data about MACLEAN'S.

<u>FOOTNOTES TO APPENDIX XVIII: CANADIAN PERIODICALS</u>, including MACLEAN'S (many other magazines are also recorded in the following Indexes)

1. CANADIAN PERIODICAL INDEX, An Author and Subject Index, Canadian Library Association, Ottawa 1988, editors Grace Heggie and 4 others for 1920 to 1937, ISBN 0-88802-187-9
-   CANADIAN PERIODICAL INDEX, 1966, (3 volumes), editor May L. Newton for 1938-1947, (1947 Dorothy Davidson), Library of Congress Catalog Card No. 62-15195
-   CANADIAN PERIODICAL INDEX, 1948-1959, edited by Isabel Bradley and 2 others, Library of Congress Catalogue Card No. 62-15195
-   CANADIAN PERIODICAL INDEX, 1960, Vol. 13, edited by Margaret Wodehouse and 1 other
-   CANADIAN PERIODICAL INDEX, 1961, Vol. 14, edited by Lenore Aedy and 3 others,
-   CANADIAN PERIODICAL INDEX, 1962, Vol. 15, edited by Margaret Wodehouse and others,
-   CANADIAN PERIODICAL INDEX, 1963, Vol. 16 - onward to 1969 edited by Margaret Wodehouse and others,
-   CANADIAN PERIODICAL INDEX, 1975, Vol. 28, editor Sylvia Morrison, Printed in Canada by Richardson, Bond and Wright Ltd. Owen Sound ISBN 0-88802-117-8, ISSN 0008-4719
-   CANADIAN PERIODICAL INDEX, 1985, Vol. 38, editor Edith Auckland, Printed in Canada by John Deyell Company, ISSN 0008-4719
-   CANADIAN PERIODICAL INDEX, 1995, Vol. 48, editor Kathryn O'Handley, Gale Canada, A Division of Thompson Canada Limited, 444 Front St. W. Toronto, ON M5V 2S9,
    ISSN 0008-4719, ISBN 1-8964116-1

2. CANADIAN POETRY, Department of English, University of Western Ontario, London, Ontario N6A 3K7

3. CANADIAN PERIODICAL INDEX 1920-1937. An Author and Subject Index, Canadian Library Association, Ottawa, 1988. Published by Canadian Library Association, 200 Elgin Street, Ottawa, Ontario K2P 1L5 Copyright (c) 1988, The Canadian Library Association, ISBN 0-88802-187-9. All rights reserved. Maclean's isn't included in this Index.

4. CANADIAN PERIODICAL INDEX. Available at Western University, London, Ontario. This index is identified only by the cover title. No other information is supplied except about the indexed periodicals and the years the periodicals were published. For example, a review of the 1928 index, all sorts of articles on pertinent subjects for studies of social services and   social welfare are included from many different periodicals.

5. CANADIAN PERIODICAL INDEX 1938-1947, printed in series A to D, E to N, O to Z. May L. Newton, Editor, Canadian Library Association, Ottawa, Canada 1966. (also ASSOCIATION CANADIENNE DES BIBLIOTHEQES) Copyright, Canada 1962. All rights reserved "permission required". Many, many magazines are included in this Index on many, many subjects. Maclean's doesn't especially stand out among all the other magazines indexed. Maclean's didn't start out as a weekly news magazine until 1978. Micro film copies of actual Maclean's magazine articles are available for reference use in the Main Public Library, London, Ontario, for 1911 to 1913, and from 1953 onward.

6. MACLEAN'S MAGAZINE INDEX, 1914-1937. The London, Ontario Library and Art Museum made this Index available to Canadian Reference librarians. Check with the London Library for actual articles which are saved in their archives. This index is about Maclean's exclusively.

7. DECADES OF SERVICE, A History of the Ontario Ministry of Community and Social Services, by Clifford Williams. Copyright, 1984 the Ministry of Community and Social Services. ISBN 0-7743-9004-2, Chapters 1 to 5.

8. MACLEAN'S MAGAZINE 1995&96, 1997, 1998 and 1999, Maclean Hunter Publishing Limited, Maclean Hunter Building, 777 Bay Street, Toronto.

APPENDIX XIX: MANAGEMENT of RECORDS, MANAGEMENT of ARCHIVES, and MANAGEMENT of INFORMATION TECHNOLOGY

The following information is from records of the Government of Ontario. The subjects are presented separately in three sub-sections. Interrelatedness of the information can't be sorted out here. Other provinces in Canada have similar historical records. With the growth and popularity in uses of the internet, provinces and municipalities, including governments in Ontario, have yet to sort out these concerns.

ARCHIVES MANAGEMENT

For my research about records management, some articles were provided to me by the Archives of Ontario. Archival works began around 1872 in Ontario. In 1903, Col. Alexander Fraser was appointed as Archivist. In 1923, the "Bureau" became the "Department" of Public Records and Archives, but the Hepburn government soon relegated the Archives to an almost fugitive position. In 1935, the Archives were transferred to the Department of Education. In 1938, it's space was greatly diminished from five floors to a small vault. Subsequently, Emergency Measures, proposed in the 1940s, drew attention to Archives; and through the 1960s, Treasury Board set up a Records Management Committee, a Records Services Branch and a Records Centre. In 1976, Management Board disbanded the Records Services Branch, and the records management programme was taken over by the Management Policy Division of the Secretariat. (paraphrased from the following sources)

SOURCES: ARCHIVARIA No. 8,(Summer 1979) "Records Management and the Ontario Archives" 1950-1976, by Barbara Craig. ARCHIVARIA No. 22, Summer 1986," 'Quaint Specimens of the Early Days': Priorities in Collecting the Ontario Archival Record, 1872-1935", by Donald Macleod.

ARCHIVIST COMMENT: "Government should ensure the availability and integrity of the information it creates or holds based on its long term value." Quoted from a speech by Ian Wilson, Archivist of Ontario, reported in OFF THE RECORD, Archives Association of Ontario newsletter.

From points of view of Canada Assistance Plan agreements, "Records" in the provinces and municipalities should be maintained for specified years to settle financial claims.

RECORDS MANAGEMENT

CONSULTANT REPORT:

"Paradoxically, the tremendous growth of government, one of the reasons supporting the initiation of a records management programme was also a factor promoting change in its structure. In general the Committee on Government Productivity recommended a decentralized structure of government to permit greater scope for individual management action, more careful separation of regulatory and operational functions, discouraging at the same time, unnecessary pre-audit control of operations." (archival, pamphlet footnote)*

*(Peter Barnard Associates, "Role, Responsibilities and Relationship of the Records Management Committee: a Report Prepared for Management Board of Cabinet".)

In 1994, by mail, Professor Douglas Hartle replied to my enquiries, about the Ontario Managagement Board of Cabinet,

> "I cannot say, of course, how Management Board approaches records management. My guess is that they view the retention of records as an administrative/legal responsibility..."

INFORMATION TECHNOLOGY MANAGEMENT

A terse statement, quoted from an IBM publication entitled DISCOVERIES, commented about technological developments since 1917 at IBM, "The IBM Canada story is a story of continual discovery and transformation. When we first opened our doors for business, timeclocks and adding machines were the order of the day. These were replaced by computers so huge that they weighed several tons and took up entire floors of office space. Now, in the age of the supercomputer, the memory available on those original computers can be stored in a chip smaller than a child's fingernail." DISCOVERIES, THE IBM CANADA STORY, G509-3003-0, Copyright IBM Canada Ltd., 1991.

A scarce supply of historical information is available with regard to means and methods of recording data and documented information about social services prior to the 1980s, and only a few comments of history can be found incidentally about the 1980s. Hyperactive, fast forward demands, in present contexts of information technology, allow scarce history. My present study doesn't attempt to sort out how information technology and history are or should be governed and/ or managed. See an outline below of Information Technology and Trends "REPORT(S)".

Short term history is being affected by ever increasingly speeded up capacities and outputs, and by metamorphoses of information technology. Some digitization technologies change overnight, bringing forth new technologies that don't download to yesterday's computers or other digitization technologies, although they can retrieve yesterday's data. While some of yesterday's technologies can't interface with new technologies at all. The industry and uses of the technologies have been described as in a revolution. It's a revolution with similarities to many historical revolutions, but it's especially different than historical revolutions.

The following review/report is about a pertinent book, TOWARD AN INFORMATION SOCIETY by Lucie Deschenes, copyright and printing by Minister of Supply and Services, Canada, edited by Canada Communications Group - Publishing, Ottawa, Canada K1A 0S9. Catalogue #C028-1/96-1992E; ISBN 0-660-14763-7

TOWARD AN INFORMATION SOCIETY, by Lucie Deschenes, defines information technology, including all electronics of sound, sight and print media in her global study, carrying readers all around the world in a sort of global inventory. The article is provoking in the questions it begs as to, What is information? Page 73 of the text provides a significant list by dates of "Major Discoveries in Computing" as follows;

1642   Blaise Pascal invents the first mechanical calculating machine (using gears).
1822   Charles Babbage develops his "analytical engine" capable of calculating logarithms.
1834   Babbage's machine becomes programmable.
1847   George Boole publishes MATHEMATICAL ANALYSIS OF LOGIC
1886   Burroughs' electromechanical adding machine.
1890   Hollerith punched card machine.
1906   First grid triodes
1928   Principle of the magnetic drum.
1932   Couffignal's binary numbering.
1937   Aiken's theory of electromechanical computers.
1938   In Germany, Professor Zuse develops the Z1, an addressable memory machine capable of performing 100,000 binary operations per second.
1941   IBM develops the MARK I, an electromechanical computer.
1943   Zuse constructs a programmable machine with 64 kilobytes of main memory.
1944   Principles of the modern computer set out by the Hungarian mathematician Von Neumann.
1949   J. W. Mauchly and J. P. Eckert construct Eniac, first electronic computer, at the University of Pennsylvania.
1950   The Edvac, first computer to use Von Neumann's architecture.
1951   First use of magnetic tape for mass storage.
1953   Magnetic core memory in ferrite.
1956   First commercial computer (Univac).
1958   Invention of the FORTRAN programming language.
1959   Univac (Sperry Rand) "Solid State I", first transistorized computer.
1960   Invention of COBOL, and Algol programming languages.
1962   Invention of real-time processing (Sperry) and time sharing (Honeywell).
1965   First minicomputer, Digital Equipment's PDP 1.
1971   IBM Series 360, first computers to use integrated circuits.
1973   Invention of the micrprocessor (Intel). First microcomputer.

RESEARCH AT THE ONTARIO GOVERNMENT LEGISLATIVE LIBRARY

A few documents through inter-library loan and through reference reading at the Queen's Park Legislative Library yielded to my research the following historical comments, here paraphrased in point form REPORT(S) -

1983 REPORT: Page #s in these notes refer to page numbers of the report. "Purpose (of a service organization) should be directly related to the objectives of a service organization and its environment and should support these objectives. An information management system which is developed either independently of the organization's objectives or in an organization with unclear objectives, is unlikely to be successful. p. 41. ..."be careful not to be swept away by technology that may not be appropriate for the organization. ("over automation")" p. 51 ...."have a technically competent advisor." p. 55. (paraphrased from INFORMATION SYSTEMS DEVELOPMENT MANAGER'S GUIDE: HUMAN SERVICES AGENCIES; 1983, published by Ministry of Community and Social Services, Management Information Services Branch & The Ontario Association of Children's Aid Societies.) It would seem from the then 1983 prescriptions of the guide, the editors anticipated the exceedingly rapid, changing environment of Information Technology of the then future 1990s.

REPORT: Management Board published reports about spending for Electronic Data Processing (EDP) for years previous to 1983-1985 based on reports from the ministries. (paraphrased from comments of the publication INFORMATION TECHNOLOGY IN THE ONTARIO GOVERNMENT 1983-1985 published by Management Board of Cabinet).

1985 REPORT: Management Board of Cabinet in Ontario issued a directive to all ministries about major information technology projects. "defined as" "a specified set of tasks with well-defined objectives and deliverables in the fields of electronic data processing, telecommunications or office automation where the estimated total facility cost is in excess of $50,000.00...."information technology - the technologies used for the creation, storage, transmission and processing of information in data, text, image or voice formats...encompases the fields of electronic data processing, telecommunications and office automation". (paraphrased from MAJOR INFORMATION TECHNOLOGY PROJECTS by Management Board of Cabinet December 1985.) The definition of Information Technology was elaborated in May 1986 as follows.

1986 REPORT: Definition of Information Technology: "the equipment, software and communications resources associated with the creation, storage, processing and communication of information in the form of data, text, image and voice. This definition includes the areas commonly referred to as data processing, personal computing, communications, and office automation." Information Technology in the 1990s is expected to be more widely used than voice communications. As opposed to analog technology, the communications industry will convert to digital technology to get advantages of software control, stored programs, and to combine voice, video and data. Custom built systems are disappearing, and users are relying on packaged software. In the rapidly changing technological environment, an Information Technology Strategy Steering Committee was created in early 1984. In May 1986, strategy recommendations were approved by the Management Board in published reports about spending for Electronic Data Processing (EDP) for years previous to 1983-1985 based on reports from the ministries. (paraphrased from STRATEGIES FOR THE MANAGEMENT OF INFORMATION TECHNOLOGY IN THE ONTARIO GOVERNMENT, as reported by the Information Technology Strategy Steering Committee, Management Board of Cabinet. May 1986.)

1986 REPORT: A publication by the Ministry of Community and Social Services noted that many internal reports were reaching different conclusions with the same data, and many other internal reports were reaching the same conclusions with different data. The publication noted that computers and information technolgy originally developed in stand-alone systems with localized impact by concerned managers, but resources of information are becoming strategic, and information technology is being introduced in an integrated manner; it's "essential that information be managed". (paraphrased from INFORMATION TECHNOLOGY STRATEGIC PLAN 1986 by the Ministry of Community and Social Services).

1988 REPORT: Information technology started cautiously in the 1950s, and large mainframe computers appeared in the 1960s and early 1970s. In the late 1970s and early 1980s, information technology shifted to medium-sized mini computers; and since the mid 1980s, there's been dramatic growth in uses of personal computers (PCs). Since 1983, more than $82 million has been spent by the Government of Ontario on purchases of 6300 PCs, including hardware and software. The trend is away from mainframe service bureaus. (paraphrased from comments of the publication INFORMATION TECHNOLOGY TRENDS REPORT 1988 published by the Management Board of Cabinet).

1991 REPORT: Personal computers (PCs) came into great demand in the 1980s, and by 1987, there was one workstation for every 7.4 employees...In 1990, the ratio became one workstation for every 2.5 employees. According to the INFORMATION TECHNOLOGY TRENDS REPORT, 1991, published by Ontario's Management Board of Cabinet

FOOTNOTES:

Footnotes are within each of the above paraphrased reports and quotations about Information Technology. Contents of the publications, which I paraphrased and quoted, are mainly descriptive or with historical significance of the short term, consistent with the fast forward modes of information technology.

APPENDIX XX: CONCLUDING REVIEWS: OTHER ARTICLES AND REPORTS

This concluding appendix reviews reports from a variety of sources. The complete reports, or parts of the reports, are reproduced here.

A copy of CANADA'S COMMUNITY SERVICE NEWSPAPER, March 1995 reported, "THE BUDGET. Block payment to replace CAP and EPF transfers, $2.7 billion less by 1997"

It was reported, major changes would occur in the federal role of financing social programs over the following two years. All transfers would be bundled into a block payment, the Canada Social Transfer (CST). The separate funding of programs under the Canada Assistance Plan and Established Programs Financing (for health and education) would end with the 1996-97 budget.

Cost sharing arrangements would end, amounts transferred would not be determined by provincial spending decisions. The new transfer would be achieved through cash payments and transfer of cash points to the provinces. Equalization payments, which benefit lower income provinces, would remain unchanged and payments would continue to grow, ensuring that all provinces can provide comparable levels of service at comparable rates of taxation.

Transfers to the provinces for social programs would drop by approximately $2.7 billion from 1994-95. The budget statement also indicated further cuts anticipated for 1997-98. To provide stability before the change, the current transfers under the present system would remain about the same.

The change to block funding includes the following:

. Provinces will no longer be subject to rules stipulating which expenditures are eligible for cost sharing;

. Administrative cost sharing will be eliminated. *

. Federal expenditures will no longer be driven by provincial decisions on the provision of social assistance and social services.

National standards will be maintained.

. The federal government will continue to enforce the principles of the CANADA HEALTH ACT. Provinces will be required to provide social assistance without minimum residency requirements.

The Minister of Human Resources will meet with provincial governments to develop a set of principles and objectives for the Canada Social Transfer.

* The above report is contradictory as to how the provinces will spend the Canada Social Transfer in each province. It stated that the federal government will not

make rules about which expenditures (of the provinces) are cost shareable. It then states that administrative cost sharing will be eliminated. Admin. costs of provinces, municipalities and of approved agencies were always part of the CAP Agreement for cost sharing. Under block funding, provinces, municipalities and approved agencies will continue to require funds for administrative costs.

CONCLUDING QUOTES FROM ACADEMIC WRITINGS

Referring again to the 1989 IPAC Journal, Volume 32, number 3, a couple of interesting articles extend into discussions about structural change, especially with regard to government expenditures.

1. "Le plan financier de la Commission Lambert"...by Mohamed Charih "Abstract: The author of this article analyses - from within the federal government - the technical, bureacratic and political difficulties the Trudeau government faced when implementing the five-year financial plan proposed by the Royal Commission on Financial Management and Accountability. The article, en francais,includes an English paragraph as an "Abstract: The author concludes that the amendments made to that plan did, upon implementation, seriously diminish the accountability role of the government with respect to Parliament" p.367.[1]

2. "Perceptions of the expenditure budget process"...by Douglas G. Hartle. "Abstract:....There were three unstated hypotheses to be tested: (tested by Hartle's article), whether political rather than technical barriers inhibit the evaluation of government expenditure programs; whether politicians are more "realistic" than bureaucrats; and whether officials, both elected and appointed, at the provincial level of government are more realistic than those at the federal level...The evidence seems to support, although obviously in a non-rigorous fashion, the first two propositions; the third is not supported." p.427.[2] (See also APPENDIX XVII, FOOTNOTE)

Douglas Hartle would need different questions about current perceptions in a new study about up-to-date "Perceptions of the expenditure budget process." (Professor Hartle died in September 1997.)

About partisan politics, it's pertinent to outline politics which have transpired since the Lambert Royal Commission on Financial Management and Accountability - Federal governments since Pierre Trudeau (Liberal) Ap'68 to Jn'79; Joseph Clark (Conservative) Jn'79 to Mr'80; Pierre Trudeau Mr'80 to Jn'84; John Turner (Liberal) Jn'84 to Au'84, Brian Mulroney (Conservative) Sp'84 to Jn'93; Kim Campbell (Conservative) Jn'93 to Oc'93;, Jean Chretien (Liberal) Oc'93-.

Ontario governments since John Robarts (Conservativew) Nv'61 to Mr'71; William Davis (Conservative) Mr'71 to Fb'85; Frank Miller (Conservative) Fb'85 to Jn'85; David Peterson (Liberal) Jn'85 to Oc'90; Robert Rae (NDP) Oc'90 to Jn'95, William Harris (Conservative) Jn'95 -.

FOOTNOTES TO APPENDIX XIX: OTHER ARTICLES AND REPORTS

1. CANADIAN PUBLIC ADMINISTRATION, The Journal of the Institute of Public Administration of Canada, Fall 1989, Volume 32, Number 3. Article by Mohamed Charish, "Le Plan financier de la Commission Lambert" p.367.

2. Ibid: Article by DOUGLAS HARTLE, "Perceptions of the expenditure budget process". p.427.

ACKNOWLEDGEMENTS

CANADA ASSISTANCE PLAN, Annual Reports; the last publication was 1993-94. Annual Reports for 1994-95 and 1995-96 will be combined in one edition. See APPENDIX VI for FOOTNOTES information. These publications have been available from the same office as are SOCIAL SECURITY STATISTICS - noted below. Information of descriptions and data are reproduced with the permission of the Minister of Public Works and Government Services Canada.

CANADIAN PERIODICAL INDEX, 200-450 Front Street West, Toronto, Ontario, M5V 1B6. See APPENDIX XVIII for FOOTNOTES information. Permission to quote from the INDEX was granted by Tania Johannsen of CANADIAN PERIODICAL INDEX.

CANADIAN PUBLIC ADMINISTRATION/ ADMINISTRATION PUBLIQUE DU CANADA. The journal published quarterly by IPAC, The Institute of Public Administration of Canada. 1075 rue Bay Street, Suite/ Bureau 401, Toronto, Ontario, Canada M5S 2B1. See the INTRODUCTION pp. 1 etc. for FOOTNOTES information. The Executive Director of IPAC gave consent to quote from the journal.

DECADES OF SERVICE by Clifford Williams. See APPENDIX XIII for FOOTNOTES information. Licence to quote from DECADES OF SERVICE is obtained from the Management Board Secretariat, Publications Ontario, Copyright Unit, 880 Bay Street, 5th Floor, Toronto M7A 1N3.

FELICITER, A Journal of the Canadian Library Association, 200 Elgin Street, Suite 602, Ottawa, ON. K2P 1L5. The editor of the periodical gave me advice as to what could be quoted from the article on "Digitization" by MacGregor Patterson, September/October 1993

Finance Minister of Canada. Printed or electronic Copies of budget technical documents are available from Distribution Centre, Department of Finance, 300 Laurier Ave. West, Ottawa, Ontario K1A 0G5. The Minister of Finance, office of the Honourable Paul Martin P.C. M.P., sent to me a package of documents concerning budget preparations and concerning speeches the Minister had made about budgets in recent years. See CHAPTER 4 for FOOTNOTED information. Information of descriptions and data are reproduced with the permission of the Minister of Public Works and Government Services Canada.

THE GREAT CODE, THE BIBLE AND LITERATURE, by Northrop Frye. Quotes are used from Professor Frye's work in most chapters and some appendices of my study here. See FOOTNOTES information among the chapters. I consulted with the President, Victoria University, in the University of Toronto, concerning rules for using quotations from Northrop Frye's works.

INFORMATION TECHNOLOGY - STRATEGIC PLANS AND TRENDS REPORTS, See APPENDIX XX for FOOTNOTES information. Consents and licences to quote from INFORMATION TECHNOLOGY reports are obtained from the Management

Board Secretariat, Publications Ontario, Copyright Unit, 880 Bay Street, 5th Floor, Toronto M7A 1N3.

NO FAULT OF THEIR OWN, by James Struthers, Published by UofT Press, 700-10 St. Mary Street, Toronto, ON. M4Y 2W8 Permission to publish my review/report was granted by the Permissions Co-ordinator, UofT Press Inc.

PRIME MINISTERS OF CANADA photos, on the inside cover, were supplied by the NATIONAL ARCHIVES OF CANADA and by the LIBRARY OF PARLIAMENT. Photos of the MINISTERS OF FINANCE on pp.65-66 were supplied by the LIBRARY OF PARLIAMENT and are reproduced with the permission of the Minister of Public Works and Government Services Canada.

PUBLIC ACCOUNTS OF CANADA, Public Works amd Government Services, Canada, Central Accounting and Reporting Sector. The Manager, Public Accounts and Finance Reporting Division authorized my quoting from the PUBLIC ACCOUNTS. See APPENDIX VIII for FOOTNOTES information. Information of descriptions and data are reproduced with the permission of the Minister of Public Works and Government Services Canada.

PUBLIC ACCOUNTS OF ONTARIO, Ministry of Finance, Ontario. Finance Ministry published the documents in recent years; since 1966, PUBLIC ACCOUNTS have also been under Treasury and Economics; Treasury, Economics and Intergovernmental Affairs; and Treasury Department was responsible for PUBLIC ACCOUNTS in earlier years. See APPENDIX IX for FOOTNOTES information. Consent to quote PUBLIC ACCOUNTS of ONTARIO is from Management Board Secretariat, Publications Ontario, Copyright Unit, 880 Bay Street, 5th Floor, Toronto M7A 1N3.

PUBLIC ADMINISTRATION IN CANADA, Selected Readings. See APPENDIX I for FOOTNOTES information. Second Edition by W.D.K. Kernaghan and A.M. Willms.

PUBLIC ADMINISTRATION IN CANADA, A Text. See APPENDIX II for FOOTNOTES information. Second and Third editions by W.D.K. Kernaghan and David Siegel. Consents to quote from the studies were given by Professor Kernaghan and Professor Siegel.

SKYWAY PRINTING, 642 12th Avenue, Hanover, ON. N4N 2V6. My sincere appreciation is expressed to Skyway Printing for careful and capable transcriptions and amendments of the manuscript with skillful uses of computerized technologies.

SOCIAL SECURITY STATISTICS, Catalogues #MT90-2/17-1993 and #MP90-2/17-1995: See APPENDIX VII for FOOTNOTES information. These volumes are supplied by the Enquiries Centre, 140 Promenade du Portage, Phase IV, Level 0, Hull, Quebec K1A 0J9. My many questions about the statistics were answered by an analyst of the Social Policy Directorate, Quantitative and Information Analysis, HRDC. Information of descriptions and data are reproduced with the permission of the Minister of Public Works and Government Services Canada.

STRAIGHT THROUGH THE HEART by Maude Barlow and Bruce Campbell. Copyright© 1995 by Maude Barlow and Bruce Campbell. See APPENDIX XIV for FOOTNOTES information. Permission for my review/report was granted by Vivien Leong, Editorial Assistant, Harper Collins Publishers Ltd, Hazelton Lanes, 55 Avenue Road, Suite 2900, Toronto, Ontario M5R 3L2

TORONTO ANNUAL ESTIMATES. Records are held at the Urban Affairs Library, Metro Hall, 255 John Street, Toronto. See APPENDIX X reference information of notes and notations. Michael Moir, Director of Corporate Records Systems and City Archivist, supplied a list of source information available, "INFORMATION ON EXPENDITURES BY THE METRO COMMUNITY SERVICES DEPARTMENT ON THE CANADA ASSISTANCE PLAN AND INFORMATION TECHNOLOGY", the list includes records which are held at the City of Toronto Archives at 255 Spadina Road, and which are supplied under application. All references were prepared by George Wharton, Archivist.

THE Y.M.C.A. in CANADA, by Murray G. Ross. See CHAPTER 4 here for FOOTNOTES information. President Emeritus, Murray G. Ross agreed to my request to include quotes and references from The Y.M.C.A. in Canada in a History of The Canada Assistance Plan. Murray G. Ross O.C LLD., President emerite, President Emeritus of York University, 2275 Bayview Avenue, Toronto, Ontario M4N 3M6.

INDEX